THE WILE BIG
DERRY PHRASEBOOK

City of Culture Edition

Seamus McConnell

GUILDHALL PRESS

ISBN: 978 1 906271 75 6

Published July 2013 by
Guildhall Press
Ráth Mór Business Park
Bligh's Lane, Derry
Ireland
BT48 0LZ
00 44 28 7136 4413
info@ghpress.com
www.ghpress.com

A catalogue record for this title is available from the British Library.

Supported by
The National Lottery®
through the Arts Council of Northern Ireland

Guildhall Press gratefully acknowledges the financial support of the Arts Council of Northern Ireland as a principal funder under its Annual Funding Programme.

For Seamus.
An inspiring daddy, a gifted brother and a
deeply missed gentleman. This is for you.
Rachael and Hugo.

Seamus McConnell
1942- 2010

Contents

FOREWORD

(Original Foreword by Seamus from last edition.)

" About 1981, because of my general interest in the history of Derry and its people, I got the idea to jot down some of the very humorous sayings unique to our city. As time went on, I began to take seriously the idea of compiling some sort of 'dictionary' of Derry words and phrases, with the vague hope of having it published some day. So around 1984, I got down to some serious research: eavesdropping on people's conversations, skulking around crowded places like supermarkets and football matches, notebook at the ready, picking up phrases here and there (wakes turned out to be a rich source of material). **Talk of the Town**, first published in 1989, was the end result of all that nosing around.

For a while I believed that I had published the cream of local expressions, but I kept hearing more and more. One day I was sitting in a local café and I couldn't help but overhear two ladies 'discussing' a neighbour's little boy and because it sounded so funny I decided there and then that a second book was a must. So **The Folly Up** was published in November 1990.

That had to be it, I thought at the time. But there was still so much out there, I couldn't help writing it all down. Collecting local patois had become almost an obsession. Every time I left the house, I found myself seeking out more. I wanted to produce a definitive 'Derry Dictionary' – **The Wile Big Derry Phrasebook** – the complete collection of Derry's very own words, phrases and linguistic peculiarities (except, of course, for those held back for the special millennium edition in 2000). After this, I swore I'd never write another book and, as Spike Milligan once said, this is it – **The Ultimate Wile Big Derry Phrasebook**. "

… Now houl on a minute! I feel anoller wan comin' on!

Or that's what we believe Seamus would be saying if he was still with us. He never did lose that obsession of eariwiggin' on people's conversations. And if he'd been around to welcome the inaugural City of Culture 2013, along with the rest of us Derry wans, he would have considered it his civic duty to ensure that all visitors to our great city would have an updated, ultimate (plus one), definitive (perhaps) **Wile Big Derry Phrasebook**. 'Cos that's just the sorta person Seamus wuz.

A naturally modest and quiet man (well, in comparison to the rest of the McConnells anyway), few are aware of the wealth of talent possessed by Mr Seamus McConnell. Not only was Seamus a prolific writer (much of his work never seen by the public eye), he was first and foremost a very gifted musician and featured heavily on the music scene in Ireland and beyond, from Showbands to Blues, from Skiffle to Jazz, from the 1950s through to the 1980s. Slowing down in his, dare we say it, more mature years, concentrating more on recording, arranging and producing, he amassed an extensive back catalogue of songs and instrumentals across all genres, again most of which has never been heard by the public ear. Indeed, one of his secret ambitions was to have some of his music used in soundtracks on the big screen. He left behind a formidable legacy, a lifetime's work.

We feel that this legacy should be preserved and made available for all to enjoy. So with this in mind a website, www.seamusmcconnell.com, archiving Seamus's work, is planned. In the meantime, however, a small sample of his music and both published and non-published works can be enjoyed at www.springtowncamp.com.

We sincerely hope you enjoy this book and it gives you as much laughter reading it as Seamus had writing it and as we had updating it. On behalf of Seamus, we would like to thank the people of Derry who were the main contributors to this book.

So put a bush in thon gap, get a wee sope in yur han' and enjoy!

Rachael McConnell-Doherty (daughter)
Hugo McConnell (brother)
July 2013

OVERHEARD CONVERSATION

Mary: De ye see if I had thon boy, ah'd draw the back a may han' across ay's ja'bone.

Sarah: Aye, ah know wat ye mean. God, ay's wile disabeejint. Wan word from ay's moller an' ay diz wat ay liks.

Mary: Lay oller day, ay putt in may wunda, ye know. See if I had a catched im, ah'd a busted ay's snotter, so ah wud. God, ah wuz ragin', so ah wuz.

Sarah: Ah don't know wat the young wans're comin' ti these days. When I wuz a wane, we'd a wee bitta thought fur wur nibbers, so way hid.

Mary: Ah, well, the sooner we git a shift from thon pliss the better. C'mon, Surra, we'd better git the rest a wur messages before the town gits black.

Sarah: Aye, ah hiv a rake ti git fur the stews fur wur tay the night.

Mary: De ye know sumfin', Surra? Lay oller day, my Shooey wuz tikkin in wi' ay's leg.

Sarah: Och, God, Murry, am wile sarry ti hear that. Wat happened ti im?

Mary: Well, ay sid ay wuz gittin' a bit of a dose, so ay went upstairs ti throw imsel down, but on ay's way up, ay slipped an' twusted ay's knee. Ay wuz roarin' outta im wi' pain, so we haddy phone the amblins an' hiv im shifted ti Altygalvin immeejitly. Ah felt a wile pity fur im an' ah hivn't an eye in may head since, so ah hivn't.

Sarah: Och, don't wurry. Sure it wuz the same wi' may moller when she fell an' horted er hench, but she wuz dead on a week lidder.

Mary: Am g'in ore the night ti see im, so am are. Wanny come wi' may?

Sarah: Naw, ah canny gore the night, Murry, but al bibbildy gore the morra evenin'.

Mary: Okey doke, Surra, see ye the morra, orr ite?

Sarah: Orr ite, Murry, see ye after.

Confused? Well read on ...

A

A Big Wane: An immature person.

A Clare Ti May Clogs: O dearie me!

A Cudda Bitt Im Wi' May Cap: Derogatory comment about cumbersome boxer.

A Fis Fur Ivry Day A The Week An' Two Fur A Sunday: Untrustworthy.

A Good Booter/Steever: A hard kick administered to another individual's hind quarters.

A Joke's A Joke But Git Yur Bum Off The Pilla: Do you not think you're carrying things a bit too far?

A Lock A Hippince: Small amount of money.

A Nairaplane: Large flying machine with wings.

A Nearly Tuk Duck Disease: I almost went into a state of shock.

A Nounch: Small measurement of weight.

A Tatchy Kis: Small case for important files, documents etc.

A Trick Above Yur Capers: Telling someone not to push their luck.

A Waitin' On: Dying.

A Wee Bit Of Fluff: Cuddly, comely maiden.

A Wee Burl Roun' The Fluer: A little episode of dancing.

A Wee Hoult: An embrace with a girl or boy.

A Wee Outins: Short trip to the seaside, nearest big city or the countryside.

A Wee Priest: Description of any young priest, regardless of size.

A Wee Scoot Over: A quick visit.

A Wee Wane In A Pram Hiz More Sense 'N' You: Why don't you grow up.

A Whole Bang Jang: An abundance of.

A Whole Hanlin': A confused and complicated situation.

A Whole Rake: A large amount of anything, exact quantity unknown.

A Wush A Wuz Ye: Aren't you lucky? I wish I was in your shoes.

A Zed: Sarcastic answer to the question, 'Why?'

A-clantic: Large expanse of water between Ireland and the USA.

Above All Days: Why did it have to happen today?

Acks: Ask.

Act Lik A Christian: Conform to accepted standards of behaviour.

Actin' The Cod: Pretending; fooling around.

Actin' The Maggot/Wack: Behaving in an annoying manner.

Actin' Up: Not playing the game; misbehaving; machinery malfunctioning.

Addig: Space in roof of house where lots of bric-a-brac are stored.

Affected: Not in control of all one's faculties.

Afflete's Fut: Medical condition causing unpleasant symptoms in the feet.

Affronted: Acutely embarrassed.

Ageein: Once more.

Ageenst: Strongly opposed to.

Agger: Argue.

Aggervittin': Causing severe annoyance and frustration.

Ah Canny: I cannot.

Ah Canny Bay Footered: I can't be bothered; it's too much trouble.

Ah Canny Git Lukin' Outta May Eyes: Gasp of despair by harassed parent.

Ah Don't See Yur Name On It: Sarcastic retort by someone who's just been accused of occupying someone else's seat.

Ah Haddy: I felt compelled to; I had to.

Ah Hadn't An Eye In May Head: Condition brought about by too much looking, reading, or too little sleep.

Ah Hivn't A Han' On May: Condition caused by person overworking.

Ah Hivn't A Sausage/Tosser: I'm financially embarrassed; completely penniless.

Ah Hivn't Got Two Hippinys Ti Rub Tigether: I'm afraid I'm a bit low on ready cash.

Ah Luv May Moller 'N' Faller: I hold my parents in high esteem.

Ah Niver As Much As Washed

May Fis The Day: I've done absolutely nothing today.

Ah Niver Did: Indignant denial that you haven't done anything untoward.

Ah Niver G'outta The Durr: I have a very uninteresting social life.

Ah Sid: I said.

Ah Suppose Al Hifty: I don't want to, but I haven't much choice.

Ah Went Up The Stairs An' Threw Maysel Down: I felt rather tired, so I went up to bed to rest for a while.

Ah Wudn't Mind A Lyin' Week Wi' That Boy: Declaration by girl that she fancies a certain young lad.

Ah Wudn't Put It Past Ye: I don't trust you; you're capable of doing something devious or underhand.

Ah Wudn't See You Stuck: Offer to help out financially, or otherwise.

Ah Wudn't Tik Ye As A Gift: You're not my type at all.

Ah Wull Jist: I certainly will.

Ah Wush: I wish.

Ahundurd: Five score.

Aikey: Awkward.

Al Giv Ye Sumfin' Ti Cry About: Threat of further punishment if child doesn't desist from crying.

Al Bibbildy Gore: I'm free to visit you later.

Al Bust Yur Clock/Snotter: I'll punch you on the face/nose respectively.

Al Crown Ye/Knock Yur Pan In: I'll inflict serious injury on your head.

Al Dance On Yur Tonsils: Threat to someone that they're about to be severely trounced.

Al Draw The Back A May Han' Across Yur Ja'bone: Dire threat by parent against child that chastisement is imminent.

Al Git Sittin' Yit: My work never seems to end.

Al Giv Ye A Week Ti Stop That: Please don't stop, I'm excited.

Al Giv Ye Two Guesses An' The First Wan Dizn't Count: You know exactly what I mean.

Al Gup An' Throw On May: I'll go upstairs and get dressed.

Al Lift Lumps Outta Ye: I can be very vicious if provoked.

Al Tell Ye Fur Why: These are my reasons.

Al Tell Ye Wan Thing, An' That's Not Two: What I'm about to say is the gospel truth.

Al Warm Yur Ear: Warning from parent to offspring to behave or else.

Alameenyum: Silvery coloured metal used for making teapots etc.

Alasayshun: Large hairy dog of German origin.

All Away Wi' Yursel: Proud; happy.

All Biz: Going about one's activities enthusiastically.

All Broke: Sheepishly embarrassed.

All Ears: Listening intently; eavesdropping.

All Pitcher An' No Soun: Frosty atmosphere prevailing when wife/girlfriend isn't speaking to husband/boyfriend (or vice versa).

All Worked Up: In a state of sexual excitement; very anxious.

Allagitter: Long fearsome reptile found in the swamps and rivers of America and Africa.

Am Are So: I am indeed.

Am Bitt: I'm defeated; I give up; I'm totally exhausted.

Am Easy: It's all the same to me.

Am Goan Out: Cheerio, I've decided to go somewhere else.

Am Niver Goney B'ble Ti Do That: Cry of desperation when failure looms.

Am Nixt: It's my turn now.

Am Not Goney Eat It On Ye: Angry retort when someone is refused permission to look at something belonging to another.

Am Not Goney Run Outta The Town Wi' It, Ye Know: Indignant retort when someone is reminded that they've got a minor outstanding debt.

Am Not Yur Skivvy: You are not the boss of me!

Am Ready Fur The Big House/ Fur Down The Strand: I think I'm going mad; I'm close to a nervous breakdown.

Am Rotton, So Am Are: I've definitely got a very bad dose of the cold.

Am Sure You're Unazy: You're not worried at all.

Am Tellin' On Ye: An angry child's threat to inform parents of another child's misdeed or displeasing actions.

Am Wile Dry: I'm very thirsty.

Am Wile Sarry: Please forgive me, I apologise.

Amblins: Emergency vehicle that transports the sick and injured to hospital.

Amup: I've arisen out of my bed.

An' All: Et cetera; and so on.

Anacordjin: Musical instrument with piano keyboard and bellows.

Annie No Rattle: One who pipes up at the end of a conversation to claim the last word.

Anniversity: Day of the year on which some important event is remembered or celebrated.

Anoller Shirt'll Do Ye: I'm afraid you're not long for this world; I can see you are not looking too healthy.

Any Danger Ay A Start? Question to a prospective employer by person not overenthusiastic about commencing gainful employment.

Any Wan Not Wearin' A Coat That Day Hasn't Got Wan: It's a bit chilly out.

Ar: Livid mark left after wound has healed.

Are Ye Rightly? I hope you're well.

Are Ye Sick? You must be joking!

Are Ye Talkin' Ti Me Or Blowin' Yur Nose/Chewin' A Breek? Said in anger when someone doesn't like the tone of another's voice.

Arkyteks: People who draw up detailed plans for houses and other types of buildings.

Arthuritus: Disease that causes pain and inflammation in the joints.

Artickilated Larry: A heavy goods vehicle.

As Big A Liar As John Green: Description of someone disinclined to tell the truth; a teller of tall tales.

As God Is May Judge: I wouldn't lie to you (even though I am).

As Good: Very kind; generous.

As Much: A lot.

As Nice As Ninepince: Phoney friendliness; insincere behaviour.

As Oul As Tay: Advanced in years; aged.

Ashy Pet: One who seldom leaves the house or who hugs the fireplace.

Ask May Bror Am I A Liar: Seeking questionable confirmation of one's honesty.

Assept: Receive thing or service offered; take on board.

Ast: Requested.

Avinyee: Tree-lined street or road (eg Beechwood Avinyee).

Aw, Dear O: Sign of exasperation.

Aw, God Luv Thim: Expression of sympathy for innocent children.

Aw, Now: We know what you're up to.

Aw, You Hiv It/Aw, Yur Mikkin' It: Your financial status is much better than you're letting on.

Aw, Wat Are Ye Talkin' About? Say no more as you're talking nonsense.

Aw, Wudn't Ye Know? Smug remark when informed of another's misdeed.

Aw Right, Hi? Good-day. How are you?

Awantin'/Awanted: Message issued loudly when a child's immediate presence is required by its parents.

Away Wi' The Donkey: Lost, whereabouts unknown.

Ay Cudn't Bliss Imsel': He was in an advanced state of intoxication.

Ay Cudn't Cure Bacon: My doctor is a bit of a quack.

Ay Fell Ore A Straw An' A Hen Keeked Im: Quip by friend about a supposedly mortally injured person when someone enquires as to how he received his injuries.

Aye: Yes.

Aye, On May Ma's Nerves: Usual answer to question, 'Are you working?'

Aye, Right Anuff: Get lost, do you think I'm an idiot?

Aye, Surely: Of course!

Dodgy Derry Diet

Modern-day fads about healthy eating and exercise seem to be a relatively new thing in Derry – as a quick glance back at old eating habits and illnesses will show. Below is a short menu, a veritable vegetarian's nightmare, of some of the local artery blockers from a few, and not so few, years ago. It's surprising there are any pigs left in Ireland at all.

Bacon Ends
General bits and pieces left over from the pig when all the good bits have been removed.

Black/White Puddin'
The main ingredient of this delicacy is blood, either from cows or pigs, with a few other dubious extras thrown in for good measure. A must for any self-respecting fry-up.

Chain Bones
From the spine of the pig (again), very popular in the preparation of soups and stews, but considered very tasty when cooked on their own.

Forced Meat
More commonly known as 'mince' but so called because slabs of meat were forced in one end of a machine and the mince emerged from the other.

Hocks
Cuts from the shank or rear end of the ubiquitous pig, usually eaten with ubiquitous chips.

Knobs/Pigs' Feet
A beautiful culinary delight when cooked with cabbage and spuds and much sought after by food experts in bygone days. In victuallers' terms, the knobs were the knuckles from the pig's feet, because pigs don't have hands, apparently.

Necks
As the name suggests, these were the neck and upper part of the pig's anatomy used in the preparation of various dishes and evidently very tasty.

Rissoles
Round flat bits of meat covered in what looked like sawdust, and made from an array of indeterminate ingredients.

Shins
The front part of the cow's leg and, apparently, flush with mouth-watering meat.

Skirts
Nothing to do with ladies' clothing, but actually the inside of a pig's ribcage. They adorned many a table on a Sunday in the forties and fifties, when, no pun intended, times were a bit on the lean side.

Special Mince
No longer known by this name but called 'hamburger meat'. James Doherty was the most famous manufacturer of this delicacy and a plentiful supply of a similar meat can still be found today.

Today's special, monsieur, is mince... on a bap

Tripe
The contents of a cow's stomach much sought after in the 'good old days' but not eaten a lot today.

Tails
No explanation needed here, so I'll explain. These could be either cows' or pigs' tails which were widely eaten years ago. I don't know how they tasted, but they must have looked strange sticking out of the pot and adorning the plate.

B

Back Return: Extension to rear of house.

Backwatter: What a person hasn't got when they speak their mind.

Bad Scran/Cess Ti Ye: I wish you all the worst.

Bad Swally: Fast eater.

Baddin: Person inclined to bouts of antisocial behaviour; mischievous child.

Badly Bent: Almost embarrassed.

Badly Stuck: Insufficient funds to carry out plans.

Bags: Lots of anything; garments covering the lower half of a man.

Baird: Hair growing on face and chin, usually on a man.

Bake: Face or mouth.

Ball A Lard: Most unkind remark about obese person.

Banana Slide: Item of recreation in children's playground.

Bang On: Just right; ideal; great.

Bankin': Steep grassy incline.

Banty: Bow-legged.

Bare Pelt: Completely naked; starkers.

Bargin' A Bucketful: Expressing grave displeasure.

Barra: Small one-wheeled cart used by gardeners and building workers.

Barred: Prohibited from entering place of entertainment because of past (mis)behaviour.

Bars: News; gossip; boyfriend or girlfriend.

Bat In The Mouth: A thump or punch in the face.

Batter On: Continue on ahead.

Batterin' Match: Overenthusiastic knocking at door; a physical confrontation.

Bayten Docket: One with all resources exhausted; situation beyond reprieve; lost bet or gamble.

Bayten Rotten: Completely overwhelmed; totally defeated.

Bealin': Festering or inflamed wound.

Beardy Nanna: Woman with superfluous hair on her face; man who always seems to have stubble.

Beat Im At The Boots: Game devised by parents to fool kids into getting undressed for bed.

Better: Having given birth.

Big An' Ugly Enough: Well able; capable of acting on one's own initiative.

Big Fis: Insult of medium seriousness; facial expression denoting huffing.

Big Long Drink A Watter/String A Misery: Tall gangly useless person.

Big Lump: Large child; ungainly person.

Big Man: One who threatens; a bully.

Big Night: Party or celebration.

Big People: Adults; grown-ups.

Big Trubbs: Serious difficulties.

Big Yank: Member of the American Forces, regardless of size.

Bile: Boil (like a pimple).

Binder: A person guilty of rash and illogical behaviour; an idiot.

Bird Mouthed: Reluctant to speak up or complain.

Bissin: Metal or plastic container for washing dishes in.

Bit Ay A Boy: Not averse to chasing the ladies; a man about town.

Bite The Nose Off: Snap at; argue with.

Bitt It Down Yur Neck: Encouragement to drink (usually alcohol) when drinker is reluctant to do so.

Bitt Ti The Ropes: Completely overwhelmed; last chance gone; penniless; drunk.

Bitta Booty: Short session of knocking a football about.

Bitta Stuff: Dubious male comment about an attractive female.

Bitter As Gall: Has an extremely tart, vinegary taste.

Bitter/Foundered/Nippin': Very cold.

Blab: Unwelcome swelling on tyre or football.

Black Bibbies: Unfortunate children of the Third World for whom collections are taken up in schools.

Blarge: Powerful but unstylish kick of a football; large amount of drink.

Blatter: Burst of gunfire.

Bleach: Hit viciously.

Bleenger: Extremely noisy passing of wind.

Bleezin': Burning vigorously.

Blellerin': Talking loudly in a moaning or complaining manner.

Blew Out: Rebuffed or rejected by the object of one's desires.

Blew Up Lik A Barrage Bloon: Having put on a few extra pounds of weight.

Bline: Unable to see.

Blissin': Benevolent bestowing of good fortune by the Almighty.

Bloon: Thin colourful plastic bag that can be filled with air and hung up as decoration at parties etc.

Blootered: Excessively inebriated.

Blurt: Disparaging name for someone not well-liked.

Bo 'N' Arra: Ancient weapon used in hunting and archery.

Bockle: Child's term for a common glass container.

Bog Yur Arm In: Take advantage of; make the best of.

Boggin': Very dirty; x-rated (of films).

Bokey/Neet: Nit or other insect infesting the scalp.

Bokeyman: Nebulous scary character from children's nightmares, usually conjured up by parents to enforce discipline.

Boller: Trouble or aggravation.

Bollerayshun: Tedious task; too much like work.

Bombed Out: All romantic connections terminated unexpectedly for no apparent reason.

Boney: Large commemorative open-air fire.

Boodles: Glass marbles.

Boot Ugly: Of a slightly less than attractive appearance.

Boul: Container for soup, porridge, etc.

Boul Brat: Impudent child.

Boul Cut: Child's hairstyle achieved by expert use of a soup bowl and scissors (usually in hard times).

Boulster: Large elongated pillow.

Boult: Type of sliding lock for door.

Boulted: Ran away hurriedly.

Boys A Boys: Exclamation of surprise and wonderment.

Brack In Ti: Enter illegally.

Brattle: Loud peal of thunder.

Brave: Good or fine as in 'a brave day'; also emphatic use as in 'brave and big'.

Breek: Lump of stone.

Brisses: Y-shaped leather contraption for holding up trousers.

Brock: Leftover household food once collected in carts and used to feed pigs.

Brockman: Man with horse and cart who collected brock.

Broke Dead/Broke Ti The Bone: Insulted, ignored or very embarrassed.

Broke Fur Ye: Sympathetic embarrassment due to the unfortunate circumstances of another.

Bru: Labour exchange; social security office.

Buck-Leppin': Jumping about in a frivolous but irksome fashion.

Bucketin'/Dashin'/Lashin'/Poarn: Raining heavily.

Bucklins: Company that runs holiday camps.

Budder: Yellow fatty substance used to spread on bread.

Budgen Hook: Buncrana train.

Bummin' Yur Load: Boasting about one's supposed abilities or achievements.

Bunnle: Bunch of material tied with string (eg bunnle a sticks).

Burl: Turn or swing round quickly.

Burnie: Very hot, therefore not to be touched.

Burry: Inter; stow away in the ground.

Burton's Dummy: Person who doesn't overexert himself; overdressed and awkward.

Bust Out: Be overcome by a paroxysm of laughing or crying.

Busty Buttons: Nickname for fat person.

Butter Wudn't Melt In Er Mouth An' A Poun' Wudn't Choke Er: She's not as innocent as she would have you believe.

Buy Now While Shops Last: Sign of the times.

STRANGE AILMENTS
PREVALENT IN THE DERRY AREA

Bile
Large, pimple-type thing which can appear on any part of the body. Not life threatening but very painful. Just one sure cure known to man and that's to stick the neck of a glass bottle filled with boiling water on to the head of it, which can't be taken off until it's been completely drawn out. Although this can cause great distress to the patient, it's always great watching it being done to some poor cratur.

Bokeys
The dread of all parents! Living creatures stomping around in their child's hair with impunity. This condition is contracted when one child who is infected comes into close contact with other children. Close contact can mean anything within a half-mile as these 'bokeys' have been known to jump at least five hundred yards. Some can grow up to a foot in length and if not tackled quickly they have been known to make a rope from the child's hair, especially if it's long, and drag them down to the quay. The most effective way to get rid of them is to shave the child completely bald and rub a mixture of Jeyes Fluid and HP sauce into the scalp three times a day and once more at bedtime.

Brongkitis
Used to be a very serious disease in times gone by but not too bad these days. It affects the lungs, causing inflammation with bouts of coughing and wheezing. Probable cause is sitting in too many bingo halls and pubs, inhaling the smoke from too many fags. In the past, removal of one or both lungs was the only cure, but nowadays it's just a matter of spending your leisure time in the smoke-free environment of the Bru.

Futrot
In the 1940s and '50, it was noticed that a lot of children were coming home from school complaining of 'wrinkly' feet. Their parents also noticed that their children's feet were very smelly and a deathly white colour. At first, doctors were sceptical about the problem but then they had to admit that the condition did exist. Although extensive research was carried out, the best medical minds of the time couldn't determine the cause of the condition. They also noticed that in some cases these symptoms were

accompanied by a painful red ring around the upper calf part of the leg. It was quite by accident that the truth of the matter was finally established when Wabbits McClean, out riding his brakeless bicycle, fell off and twisted his ankle. At the hospital, the doctors struggled to get his boots off, and when they finally did, they discovered he was in an advanced state of futrot. It was then that it finally struck them and they discovered the cause of this chronic complaint: ill-fitting water boots that were letting in!

Gammy Leg

This disease seems to be endemic to professional footballers, and particularly to ones in the Brandywell area. In the majority of cases, it only affects one leg, but it can strike at both and when it does the results can be disastrous. Diagnosis of the condition can be tricky, but the general medical consensus seems to indicate that anyone suffering from the disorder appears to display an inordinate inability to run or kick a ball. It also seems to impair their sense of direction, making it almost impossible for players, especially the front runners, to find the goalposts. Various cures, such as frequent sacking of managers, resignations of directors and so on, have been tried, but apparently with little or no success. A new treatment has recently been tried, but that, too, seems to have failed. It involves bringing in players from all arts and parts, like Ballybofey, Omagh or Nigeria, letting them play for a week or so and then packing them off back home again. This extreme remedy has also failed miserably to halt the insidious progression of the disease. The only possible answer seems to be prevention, and that means a thorough scan on the GOAL (Gamminess Of A Leg) detector machine, and hopefully the disease will be identified early enough for it to be treated successfully.

The Gimmeys

This disease is found mainly in children but can affect adults as well. The strange thing about it is that it can cause greater pain to the people around the patient than the patient him/herself. The main symptoms to watch for are the incessant nerve-racking demands of the patient crying, 'gimme this' or 'gimme that', and the inevitable huffing in the corner if he/she doesn't get what he/she wants. If left unchecked, the child could be murdered. There's only one tried and tested cure, and that's to swathe the child's head in plaster of Paris and feed him/her intravenously.

Light Head
This condition causes the patient to stagger and stumble about all over the place and generally make a nuisance of himself. For a long time, the cause was unknown, but then they realised that it was brought on by too much air getting in through the ears. After discovering that, the cure was simple: wear earmuffs.

Mad Cab Disease (MCD)
This is a serious disorder that seems to turn the sufferers into deranged monsters. The disease is confined almost exclusively to taxi drivers, and it has almost reached epidemic proportions. The first symptoms are a tendency to cause traffic jams and block whole streets, especially Sackville Street and William Street, with 15-year-old Nissan Bluebirds or brand-new Vauxhall Cavaliers. As the disease progresses, far more serious symptoms may manifest themselves, such as an irresistible urge to blare horns in the middle of the night and a complete 'mental blindness' to the existence of other road users. In extreme cases, more deadly signs, like driving along footpaths and driving out of side streets without stopping, may appear.

The Jandies
Moderately serious condition caused by malfunction of the liver and brought on by certain other medical conditions. Can also be triggered by the disgusting behaviour of some individuals, like blowing their nose onto the street, hence the expression, 'You give me the jandies' (symptoms may include a yellowing of the skin).

The Pip
A disconcerting mental disorder instigated by the childish and infuriating behaviour of people with whom the sufferer just happens to disagree. It spurs the patient to assail the offending individual with a tirade of abuse by hurling uncomplimentary statements such as 'You sicken my happiness' or 'You're a mouth, so ye are' at the person concerned. In most cases, the condition is only temporary, but unfortunately in some it can be

permanent; my advice is to stay well clear of anyone afflicted by this nasty illness. A cure can be effected by just being very nice to the patient.

The Skitters
A looseness of the bowels necessitating swift and frequent sojourns to the loo. Probably caused by the consumption of too many fries or curries. Can be most alarming for the sufferer and the general public alike if an attack occurs in the city centre, where toilets are few and far between. They say that eating an Oxo cube helps. It doesn't actually cure it but can thicken it up a bit. Alternatively, bicycle clips can be worn.

Tillophobia
This is one of those little-understood mental disorders that only seems to afflict certain sections of the population, in this instance, supermarket checkout girls. The symptoms aren't difficult to recognise. The first indication that something is wrong is whenever shoppers waiting in the queue suddenly engage in protracted sighing and shuffling of feet, as the girl at the checkout seems to have downed tools in order to discuss the previous night's 'craic' at the disco with her colleague at the adjacent till. This phase can sometimes be curtailed by one of the shoppers threatening to call the manager 'if she doesn't shut er bake'.

The second stage of the illness may then set in, with the checkout girl's face assuming a strange, vacant expression as all the people in the queue collectively receive a telepathic message from the victim which says: 'I hit this job, so I'm goin' ti mik youse suffer, so am are.' This stage in the illness is usually followed by the patient abruptly disappearing from the scene altogether, to return five minutes later when the agitation in the queue has turned to open hostility with lots of cursing and swearing. In the final stages of this disorder, the checkout girl may suddenly declare to the seriously exhausted shoppers standing in the queue with their bulging trolleys: 'This desk is now closed. Move on down, please.' She then pulls a chain across the passageway and stomps off, causing a near riot as trolleys, baskets and shoppers scramble to the nearest, shortest queue, where, inevitably, the till roll has just run out …

Wakeness

A sudden feeling of being unwell with symptoms like dizziness and shaking. It can be physical or brought on by an attack of nerves. If confronted by someone who's having an attack, do not tell them to 'Wise up' or 'Git a grip, wud ye' or you'll only make matters worse. The best thing to do is to take them to the nearest pub and fill them full of brandy. This should calm them down a bit and alleviate the symptoms. If this doesn't work, threaten to tell the Electricity Board that they're fiddling the meter. This should do the trick.

Wanderin' Han' Syndrome (WHS)

This illness is mainly confined to the male of the species, although it's reported that on rare occasions females can suffer from it, too. The first person to notice the symptoms is usually the patient's girlfriend when she suspects that her boyfriend's hand is beginning to move tentatively towards forbidden areas of her person. If nipped in the bud by the lady administering a good slap in the bake to the offender, there will usually be no more problems. If, however, due to the lady's unwillingness to cause embarrassment, or worse, get dumped, the condition is allowed to get out of control, and once the offending limb reaches a certain area, I'm afraid the disease has become incurable.

Watterbrash

This is a digestive disorder where the sufferer is plagued by constant bouts of heartburn accompanied by the spewing up of an acid-filled clear fluid. The sufferer usually spits the foul-tasting liquid into the fire, which causes a massive flame to flare up and at times was such that it kept the house warm all night. The most severe case was reported to be a man from the Creggan Heights area who is said to have brought up the biggest watterbrash on record, although it's not officially recognised by the Guinness Book of Records. Apparently, it was around a gallon and a half.

Wile Dose a Coul

This is a relatively minor ailment but can have an assortment of unpleasant symptoms such as a snottery nose, and germ-laden bouts of sneezing and coughing. In extreme cases, when the patient complains of 'feelin' cat' or 'wake as watter', other symptoms may appear such as 'slabbers'. Unfortunately, there is no known cure, but sometimes taping a jar of Vicks to the sufferer's nose helps alleviate the symptoms.

Derryman undergoing the new DLA (Disability Living Allowance) test.

Swilly Bus launches new eco-friendly service.

BREEZE-BLOCK BUSTERS QUIZ

The letters inside the breeze-blocks below correspond to the initials of the words in the answers. So, if the letters were **ADD** and the clue was 'How far is it to Buncrana?' – the answer would be '**A Day's Dander'**. Easy peasy! All the answers are sayings close to a Derry wan's heart.

1. **WYND** – Stop complaining!
2. **ABGB** – A somewhat timid male
3. **YHAM** – Tell someone they're talking rubbish
4. **AOM?** – Solicit stranger for money
5. **YGWD** – Expression of disbelief
6. **YSNSTLN** – Unkind remark about a family member
7. **AYAWA?** – Reply to idle threat
8. **LS** – Highly improbable
9. **GHWY** – Offer to share a financial burden
10. **SNTYSC** – Sound legal advice
11. **UATIR** – Whereabouts classified
12. **ALAC** – Behave yourself
13. **ATOY** – Child informer's threat
14. **ADAAS?** – Unenthusiastic enquiry about work
15. **DBTTYB** – Get a move on
16. **GYHS** – Find tranquillity
17. **IDBMCT** – I will say this only once
18. **WYBIAF?** – Close the door, please
19. **ATC** – Fooling around
20. **FPTY** – Comment on clever action
21. **IHYU** – Take legal action against someone
22. **JS** – Prominent Derry politician

C

C'meer A Wee Minute: To attract someone's attention with a view to telling them something secret or important.

C'meer But Hi: On second thoughts.

C'meer, Hi: Would you mind coming over here as I want to talk to you?

Cacky: Dirty; light admonition to child not to touch.

Calendar: Container full of holes for straining food.

Can't Houl Yur Watter: Unable to keep a secret; indiscreet.

Can't See Fur Lukin': Staring ignorantly.

Can't Thole: Unable to stand or tolerate

Cannel: A candle.

Car On: Go on about your business.

Carrigan: Light, casual woollen jacket.

Carryin': Having surplus money on one's person.

Cat Melojin: Terrible; really bad.

Cat: Very bad; disappointing.

Cat's Fur, Did Ye Iver See It On A Dog? Sarcastic answer to the question, 'What for?'

Catch Yursel On: Come to your senses; don't be silly.

Catch: Not as good as it's made out to be; a con trick.

Catched: Caught red-handed; taken for a ride.

Catchin' Flies: Standing with your mouth open looking surprised.

Catlick: Non-Protestant.

Certint: Absolutely sure.

Champ: Mixture of bread and tea.

Chancer: Sly person; a conman.

Change Yur Tune: Adopt a different attitude.

Change Yursel: Put on a new set of clothes.

Chawin': Eating noisily.

Cheesed Off: Fed up.

Cheevy: Chase; run after.

Chessy: Fruit of the chestnut tree used for playing conkers.

Chest Lik A Fourpenny Rabbit: A bit on the thin side.

Chimley: That part of the house which allows smoke from the fire to escape.

Chinstrap: Black ring around child's neck caused by failure to wash.

Chip John: Any business man who overcharges.

Chipper: Not as costly; less expensive.

Chiss: Pursue; run after; see off pronto.

Chissin' It: On the hunt for a wife; engaged in courtship.

Choon Gum: Obnoxious sticky stuff chewed by people of a nervous disposition.

Chuck It Out: Desist immediately, you're annoying me.

Civil Bein': Well-mannered agreeable sort of person.

Clap: Cowpat; heap of cow dung.

Clean Mit Niver Fattened A Pig: Admonishment to person who's over-particular about food hygiene.

Cleared: Ran off; disappeared.

Click: To succeed in romance.

Clove Fut: The trademark of the devil, allegedly appearing to poor unsuspecting humans from time to time.

Clows: Your everyday apparel.

Clows Paig: Little wooden (or plastic) object used for securing clothes onto a clothesline.

Coffin Nails: Old fashioned brands of strong cigarettes.

Come Easy, Go Easy, God Send Sunday: Description of laid-back, not easily ruffled type.

Comin' Back Ti Yursel: Looking better; more like your old self.

Complint: Objection, either verbal or written.

Conscrew: Apply a meaning to someone's words at variance with what was intended.

Conshume: Eat entirely.

Contrary: Awkward; obstinate; argumentative.

Coo-Coo: Hello, here I am (usually addressed to child).

Cooert: Place where legal disputes are settled by a judge, and sometimes a jury.

Cooter: Face.

Corinthian Crawl: Type of shuffling dance supposed to have originated in the old Corinthian ballroom.

Corned Beef Tin: Small community centre in Creggan Estate, Derry.

Corner Boy: Layabout; one who loiters around the streets all day.

Corns: Currants.

Corp/Tube: Derogatory name for a useless person.

Corporation Hair Oil: Tap water used for hair styling when times were hard.

Coul: Not warm.

Coul Rife/Ye've No Blud In Ye: Said of/to someone who's always complaining about the cold.

Coul Showlder: What you get when you're completely ignored; a brushoff.

Coul Snotter: Description of someone ignored, abandoned or stood up.

Cozzie: Half a brick or large stone.

Crab: Argument provoker; disgruntled type.

Crabbit: Bad-tempered; irritable.

Craic's Ninety: We're having a jolly good time.

Cran': Machinery for lifting heavy loads.

Cribbin': Moaning or complaining.

Crissanin': Church service where baby is given its name by having water poured on its head.

Cruddles: Curdled milk spat out by babies.

Cruel: Very bad; hard to take (as of performer).

Crummles: Particles of bread.

Crunnion: Head.

Cryin' Jas/Oul Cryba: One who is easily upset or complains for no reason; weepy child.

Cuckle: Having an impediment of eyesight.

Cud Be Heard At Doho: Very loud.

Cudn't Git Over: Amazed; unable to comprehend the situation.

Culchie: Anybody who doesn't live in Derry.

Curly: Type of vegetable.

Curly Watter: Mixture of sugar and water supposed to make hair curl.

Cuttelry: Knives, forks, spoons, etc.

D

Dake: Small sum of money given back to unlucky gambler.

Dale: Distribute cards out to card players.

Damned Apt: Appropriate; totally right or fitting.

Dancin': Hopping mad with rage.

Dander At Yur Cush: Stroll at your leisure.

Daygeller: All at the same time; in a group.

De Ye? Do you?

De Ye Know You're Livin'? For God's sake, shake yourself.

De Ye Want Jam On It? There's no satisfying you.

Dead Chip: Not very dear.

Dead If Ye'd The Wit Ti Stiffen: Not looking too well.

Dead Nip: Mysterious black mark appearing overnight on body.

Dead On: Just great; giving satisfaction.

Dead On, Dickie Valley: I don't quite believe you, sir.

Dead Soldier: Empty Guinness bottle, contents just been drunk.

Deadly: Great; to be admired.

Death On: Very much opposed to.

Debtor: Creditor.

Ded'ner: A person to be wary of.

Deef: Hard of hearing.

Deep: Mysterious; descriptive of someone who thinks a lot.

Desprit: Terrible.

Deuce: Two pennies; tuppence in 'old' money.

Devalve: Give up; stop talking; be quiet.

Dew Points: Large American chemical factory based at Maydown outside Derry.

Dial: Face.

Dickied Up/Dolled Up/Dressed Up Ti The Nines: Stepping out in style; a picture of sartorial elegance (usually in preparation for a special event).

Diddin Ah? Didn't I?

Diddly Dee: Light-hearted reference to Irish music.

Die Wi' That Face An' Nobody'll Wash Ye: Cheer up! Don't be so downhearted or you'll put people off.

Die Wi' Yur Leg Up: Go down fighting.

Diffrint: Not the same; unalike.

Diktittin': Laying down the law in no uncertain manner.

Dilly Pippers: The newspapers which are produced each day.

Dinty/Wee Low Set: Small in stature; petite.

Dirty Baste: Immoral or unclean character.

Dirty Butter: Person who seldom washes.

Dirty Luk: Facial expression of disapproval.

Disabejince: Child's unwillingness to do as instructed.

Discomboberate: Confuse; destroy; dismantle; completely annihilate.

Disease: Description of obnoxious person.

Disgriss: Utter shame.

Dissint Oul Spud: Kind, generous person (not necessarily old).

Dit: Time of the month.

Ditt: Romantic rendezvous with member of the opposite sex.

Divilmint: Petty mischief; tomfoolery.

Divour: Violently take to task; severely reprimand.

Diz It Annoy Ye? Why don't you mind your own business.

Diz Yur Sister Tell Ye Ivryhing? Smug retort when being teased about being a womaniser.

Do As You're Bid: Request to obey.

Do The Pliss Up: Redecorate the house.

Do Wat The Bees Does – Buzz: Command to go away.

Do Ye Hink I Came Up The Foyle In A Bubble? I'm not as naive as you may think.

Do Ye Want A Medal? Sarcastic reply to boaster.

Dobbin'/Sconcin': Staying away from school without consent.

Dock Horney: Harbour policeman.

Doesn't Miss A Bar: Knows everything that is going on; a nosey person.

Dogged: Mean; nasty; unfair; unnecessary act.

Doin' The Dog: Causing disappointment; playing a dirty trick on someone.

Doings: Catch-all word for any forgotten item.

Don't Be Sarry, Jist Be Careful: I wouldn't do that again if I were you.

Don't Be There Till Yur Back: Hurry up; be quick.

Don't Darken The Durr: Never go there again; stay well away.

Don't Keek That Cap, There's A Man Under It: He's a bit on the small side; jovial remark about a person's stature.

Don't Sicken May Happiness/ Go An' Scratch: Don't bother me; leave me alone.

Don't Spend It All In The Wan Shop: Facetious advice given to recipient of paltry sum of money.

Don't Stan' Sideways Or Ye'll Be Reported Missing: Unkindly remark to thin person.

Don't Start May: I'd advise you to shut up; be wary of asking me that.

Don't Tik Im On: Advice given to ignore someone who may be annoying.

Done Ti The Two Eyeballs: Grossly overcharged; swindled.

Donkeys: A long time.

Doof: Beat up; assault.

Dooter: Lag behind; dally aimlessly.

Dootsie: Old fashioned; corny; childish.

Dotter: Female offspring.

Double Week: Fortnight's dole money, family allowance or wages, depending on circumstances.

Down Ti Budgen: Up to Buncrana.

Dragged Up: Badly reared by parents.

Dragon: Not exactly the most attractive person in the world.

Drooth: Acute, almost unquenchable, thirst.

Drowneded: Completely soaked by heavy rain.

Dry Up/Dry Up An' Blow Away: Forceful request to stop talking; I can't stand you so shut up and leave me alone.

Dry Yur Eyes/You're Sorely Wrought: Stop moaning or complaining, will you!

Duckle: A gormless or cowardly person.

Dunt: To thump.

Durdy: Not very clean; messy.

Durr: Entrance to a home or other building.

Durrhannle: Metal or wooden appendage on door to assist opening and closing.

Durrstep: Thick slice of bread.

Dyin' About: Very fond of.

Dyin' Lukin': Physical condition giving cause for concern.

E

Easy Goin' Tam: A calm individual; not easily ruffled.

Eat/Eat The Fis A/Rare Up On: Violently take issue with; scold; give off to.

Edyemicated: Well-versed in matters academic; very smart.

Eejit: One who engages in clownish acts; a buffoon.

Effin' An' Blindin': Swearing profusely.

Ekker: Homework.

Elected: Situation where the required result is likely.

Ellafint: Large animal with long nasal appendage and outsized ears found in India and Africa.

Empy: Not full; to beat someone up.

Even The Dogs In The Street Know: It's common knowledge.

Evenin': Afternoon.

Exkip: Flee; get away from captivity.

Extree Mungshun: Anointment of a person on their death bed by a priest with holy oils.

Eyday: Six dozen and eight.

Eye Ye Away? (So's The Smell): Friendly words of departure.

Eye Ye Gan Out? Invitation to girl to dance by hopeful suitor.

Eye Ye Outta Yur Scon Ur Wat? Have you taken leave of your senses? That's a very inadvisable course of action.

Eye Ye Paralysed Ur Wat? Do your own work, you lazy sod.

Eye Ye Practisin' Fur Santa Claus Ur Wat? I see you're cultivating a beard.

Eye Ye Whalin' Away? Are you still going strong?

Eye Ye? Are you?

WHO WANTS TO BE A 2013 CULTURE VULTURE?

In the year that's in it – City of Culture 2013 – Derry wans are being inundated with 'culture' from all arts and parts. So try this short quiz to see if you would qualify as a Culture Vulture (and maybe get your hands on one of them grants!)

1. By what name was the city first known?
A Doire Colmcille
B Doire City FC
C Legenderry United
D Thon hill over there, beside that big river

2. Which saint wrote the first biography of Colmcille?
A St Bernard
B St Andgreavsie
C St Adamnan
D St Johnstone

3. Which king laid siege to Derry in 1688?
A King Kong I
B King Wil.i.am
C King James II
D King Edward potato

4. Which gate did the Apprentice Boys shut in 1688?
A Ferryquay Gate
B The garden gate
C Hell's gates!
D Watergate

5. Who, or what, does the skeleton on the city's coat of arms represent?
A Chris DeBurgh
B Pirates of the Caribbean
C Sir Walter DeBurgo
D A big dog's dinner

6. Where was Derry's first town hall built?
A Du Pont
B Strabane
C The Diamond
D Ikea

7. What does the city's motto Vita Veritas Victoria mean?
A Gran' wee town
B Life, Truth, Victory
C All greyhounds welcome
D Hurry up, Victoria, taxi's waiting!

8. Where was Derry's first gasworks?
A Guildhall Council Chamber
B Brandywell Stadium
C Public toilets in Waterloo Place
D Bridgend ('cause it was cheaper there)

9. What did the initials BSR stand for?
A Big Shiny Records
B Birmingham Sound Reproducers
C Binlids, Stone-throwers and Riots
D Bogside Scouts Regiment

10. What was the name of Dana's 1970 Eurovision winner?
A Diva
B All Kinds Of Everything
C A Whole Hanlin'
D Teenage Kicks

11. Who makes the best stews?
A Yur Ma
B Yur Ma
C Yur Ma
D Yur Ma

Answers on a postcard, please, and send to: You, Your House, Where You Live, Your Post Code. Don't forget to put a telephone number in case you need to get in contact with yourself. Winners will receive a postcard in the post. Or maybe they won't. Losers will get one too!

The Ten Commandments – Derryman Style

1st – Thou shalt call the city by its true name, either Derry or Londonderry, not that most derisive of terms, 'Stroke City'.

2nd – Thou shalt support thy team each week at the Brandy by shouting abuse at the man dressed in black with a whistle (not the nearest clergyman).

3rd – Thou shalt not get caught working and drawing the Bru.

4th – Thou shalt not tap off yur ma (except on Friday nights for a few 'swallys').

5th – Thou shalt not covet thy neighbour's greyhound, pigeon, or new satellite dish.

6th – Thou shalt wait in the car reading the Tilly outside Tescos while the wife does the shopping.

7th – Thou shalt eat two baps a day, minimum.

8th – Thou shalt not signal when driving, especially at roundabouts.

9th – Thou shalt 'besport' thyself in white socks and a 'tache at every opportunity.

10th – Thou shalt walk thy greyhound twice a day (except when it's raining).

11th – Thou shalt learn to work out, to the nearest wing, a 50p reverse forecast 'Yankee'.

12th – Thou shalt buy thy petrol over the border when getting yur lotto.

13th – Thou shalt not tell your better half she looks fat in anything (unless she does!)

14th – Thou shalt never admit you are lost whenever you foolishly decide to venture out of your beloved city – ever!

F

Fadin' Away Ti An Ellafint: Putting on weight.

Failed: Having lost weight; sick looking.

Fair Chanter: Good singer.

Fair Doos: Good luck to you.

Fair Lukin' Haff: Very good-looking woman.

Fair Play Ti Ye: Didn't you do well? Congratulations.

Fairly: Flexible measurement of size, speed, time, etc., as in 'fairly moving' or 'fairly big'.

Fall In Ti Beef: Put on weight.

Fall In Wi': Meet; join up with.

Fall Out Wi': Cease to be on talking terms with a friend.

Faller: Male parent.

Famous Fur: Infamous for; having a bad reputation.

Fancy Yursel: Imagining (wrongly) you're a big hit with the opposite sex.

Far Out As Kit Logue: Wrong; way off the mark.

Far Shuk: Health badly deteriorated; changed for the worse.

Far Thru: Confused; in a muddle.

Fe Ye: For you.

Feardy Cussderd: Easily scared; timid person; coward.

Feared: Afraid; scared.

Febuwurry: Second month of the year.

Fihnt: Pass out; lose consciousness.

Filums/The Shows: The pictures; the movies.

Fingery Friel: Clumsy, fidgety person.

Fire Maygade: Body of men dedicated to extinguishing unwanted fires.

Fis: Face.

Fis As Long As The Day An' The Morra: Down in the dumps; sorry for oneself.

Fis Lik The Back Ay A Bus/A Busted Boot: Very ugly; not good-looking.

Fishie: Establishment that sells fish and chips.

Fissin'/Fernenst: Positioned opposite; face to face.

Fisslin': Soft scratching sound; sound of light movement.

Fissy: Light insult.

Flake It: Fall asleep; faint or die.

Flash The Ash: Hand round cigarettes.

Flay: Flea.

Floot Me: Oath used by the meek.

Fluer: Inner lower surface of a room.

Flume: Polite swear word.

Fly Man: Crafty fellow; not to be trusted.

Flyer/Flyin' Machine: A person (or thing) that moves at great speed (but not a plane).

Flyin': Doing well; very successful.

Folly: Tag along behind.

Folly Up: Pursue to conclusion; a sequel.

Footerin': Tinkering or messing about; using delaying tactics.

For'ner: Person from another country; alien.

Forbye: As well; also.

Fordy: Three dozen and four.

Fork: Opening at front of trousers.

Forrid: Part of head just above the eyebrows; about to be punished (as in 'you're forrid now').

Forty Coats: Name given to person who's 'over-clothed'.

Fraud The Beetle: A cheat.

Frens: People who can be relied on.

Frigfiss: Unpleasant name for disliked person.

Frill: Feeling of excitement.

From Flagfall: From the very start.

Frosty Face: Joker in pack of cards.

Full Ay 'Imsel: Preoccupied with his own self-importance.

Full: Drunk and incapable.

Fulla Wun: Inclined to suffer from flatulence.

Fur The Altar: About to receive communion in church.

Furgit: Fail to remember.

Furiver: Everlasting; eternal.

Futpad: Pavement.

Futrot: Disease brought on by waterboots letting in, so causing feet to look shrivelled and white.

G

G'In Indy Libber: Entering the last stages of pregnancy.

G'On A That Wi' Ye: Be off with you; tell that to the marines.

G'On An' Git Haffa Ton A That Dirt Aff Ye: I think it's about time you had a wash.

G'On Giv Is A Wee Tist: May I have some, please?

G'On Lik: Act in a similar manner; emulate.

Gab: Country dweller.

Gack: Stupid, awkward-looking person.

Galler Up: Term for band or football team just thrown together in a hurry, usually for one performance only.

Galler: Collect together (eg galler flowers).

Gammy (Leg): Lame or limping.

Gang-gureen: Serious disease causing rotting of the limbs.

Gansey: Pullover; jumper; expression of approval.

Gayvel: End wall of house.

Geek: Lacking in looks and personality; dullard.

Germans: Paris buns.

Gern The Weller: One who moans about the climatic conditions.

Get: Derogatory name for someone.

Gimme A Hot Connection: Have you a light?

Gimme Head Peace: Stop annoying me.

Gimme Yur Dandie: Request from mother to child to take her hand.

Git A Grip/Git A Grip On Yur Underwear: Please try and bring yourself under control.

Git A Man In: Employ someone to do household repairs or decorations.

Git A Shift: Be allocated a new house.

Git A Start: Find employment.

Git A Wee Run Roun': Pay a quick visit.

Git Aff An' Push It: Jibe directed at cyclist, especially if bicycle is old.

Git Aff Yur Mark: Be accepted by member of the opposite sex as a companion for the night.

Git Away A That Wi' Ye: I don't believe you.

Git Away: You don't say.

Git Fixed Up Wi': Establish a romantic link with.

Git In There An' Say I Sent Ye: Term of self-congratulation.

Git In There, Norton: Didn't I do well?

Git Off Ye: Get undressed.

Git Off: Close encounter with the opposite sex, usually at a dance/disco.

Git On Ye: Get dressed.

Git Ontay: Take issue with or reprimand someone about their actions.

Git Out The Good Cups: The priest's coming to visit.

Git Scripped: Go away; you're not on.

Git Shot: Go away; take yourself off.

Git That Durr: Please answer the door.

Git The Bars Wi': Assume a position of girlfriend or boyfriend.

Git The Haff: Have an unexpected afternoon off school.

Git The Worst Word In Thur Mouth: Be subjected to intense verbal abuse.

Git Up Them Stairs (Or I'll Buy A Bungalow): Isn't life wonderful?

Git Yur Feet Under The Tibble: Be invited round to girlfriend's house (regarded cynically as the first step towards marriage).

Git Yur Foda Tuk: Have your photograph taken.

Git Yur Head Shired: Get away from it all; find peace.

Git Yur Length: Eventually get around to visiting someone.

Git Yur Pot Scripped: Go to the confessional box to declare past misdeeds.

Git Yur Rag Up: Muster some courage; get angry.

Gitt: Entrance to field.

Gitta Houlta: To find eventually after a long search.

Gitta Lenna: Borrow for a short period of time.

Gittin' As Big: Growing up.

Gittin' At: Directing one's remarks at somebody while indirectly criticising another.

Gittin' Hung: About to enter a state of wedded bliss.

Gittin' Wile Oul: Approaching the latter stages in life.

Gittin' Wile Stout: Putting on weight (usually as a result of being pregnant).

Giv That Man A Food Parcel: 'Award' offered to male who's just announced how gallant or brave he's been.

Giv Is Share: Give me some.

Giv Im A Bib: Isn't he a sloppy eater?

Giv Is A Bitta That Heat: May I have a seat at the fire, please?

Giv That Fluer A Lick: The floor needs washing.

Glar: Thick oozy mud.

Glassy Pipper: Material that Lucozade bottles used to be wrapped in; cellophane.

Gleed: Glimmer of light in fire; an idea.

Gleek: Quick look, often sneakily.

Glengorm: Dirt; muck.

Go A Wee Run: Set off on a short spin in a car.

Go Ahead, Back Away: Somewhat confusing instruction to vehicle driver to commence reversing.

Go An' Tik A Runnin' Jump Ti Yursel: Uncompromising term of refusal.

Go An' Boil Yur Head: Disgusted refusal of a request; definitely not.

Go Haffers: Share equally among two friends (usually when finances are low).

Go Home, You're Naked/ Yur Moller Wants Ye: Friendly banter directed towards football opponents.

Go On Yur Neck: Stumble or fall.

Go Roun' Meg's Ti You: It's difficult to get you to understand anything; you're basically stupid.

God Bliss The Mark: Expression of sympathy for one afflicted with illness or disablement.

God Bliss Iss An' Save Iss: May the Almighty have pity and protect me.

God Forgive Ye: Reproach for speaking ill of someone; expression of horror at another's irreverence.

God Furgimmey This Day: Asking the Lord for absolution for speaking ill of someone (usually in no uncertain terms).

God Luk Ti Ye, Thur's Not A Pik On Ye: Wry comment passed when grossly overweight person complains about the necessity to eat.

God Luk Ti Yur Wit: You're naive; you haven't much chance of success.

God, Youse Are Good Ti Yursels: Criticism of overindulgent individuals.

God's Gift: Chauvinist male with delusions of grandeur.

Goin' Spare: At wits' end; cracking under pressure.

Gone On: Request to proceed.

Goney: Going to; about to.

Good Man, Yursel: Well done, old chap.

Good Steam: Funny; humorous; enjoyable.

Good Thing: Horse or greyhound most likely to come in first; female of dubious morality.

Good Tist: A fair amount, exact quantity unknown.

Googy: Vision slightly askew; not 20-20 eyesight.

Goose Gab: Bitter fruit.

Gorbal: Person from the Waterside district of Derry.

Gout: To exit the premises.

Gover: Go over.

Gover Yur Notes: To lecture someone at length.

Govvermint: People elected to (supposedly) run the country.

Govvermint Artist: One who claims (or 'draws') unemployment benefit.

Grab A Sit: Please take a chair.

Gran': Feeling healthy, fit or well.

Gravy Ring: Doughnut with a hole.

Grazy: Greasy, usually of chips.

Great Wi': On very friendly terms with.

Greatest Thing Since Flemin's Baps/Dordy's Mince: Best invention ever.

Gripps: Sweet fruit of the vine used for making wine.

Gritt: Part of fire that holds the coal in place.

Grittin': Metal covered hole along end of footpath to allow water to drain away.

Grodda: Shrine containing statue of the Virgin.

Growin' Lik A Cow's Tail: Getting smaller; growing downwards.

Grunter: Incompetent footballer.

Gub: Mouth.

Guilthall: Large ornate building where Derry City Council used to sit.

Gulderin': Roaring or shouting.

Gulf: Refined game played with clubs, balls, tees and holes.

Gulpin: Ill-mannered person; one devoid of breeding.

Gumbile: Painful inflamed swelling in mouth.

Gummy: Unkind remark about person short on teeth.

Gunder: Go below.

Gunga Din: Good-humoured nickname for a friend.

Gunk: A setback or surprise.

Gup: Ascend (eg gup the stairs).

H

Hacker: A footballer whose kicking is not confined to the ball.

Haff-A-Dollar: 12½ new pence; 2s. 6d. in 'old' money.

Haff-A-Man: Derogatory appraisal of a male.

Haff Ra': Not very well cooked.

Hage: Row of bushes between fields or gardens.

Hair: Fight between females with a view to extracting some hair from opponent.

Hairy Wane: Person older than they appear.

Hallion: A rough character who behaves coarsely at times.

Hammered: Exhausted; unlucky; heavily defeated; drunk.

Han' Lik A Fut: Oversized appendage; a bad hand at cards.

Hangin' From May Upper Lip: Sarcastic answer to someone inquiring after another's location.

Hanted: Acting or looking strange, unusual or downright weird.

Hard As Goats' Knees/Knap Stones: Very tough.

Hard Ti Whack: Just great; unbeatable.

Hard Ticket: Tough character; a good street fighter.

Harmlis Critter: One who wouldn't hurt a fly; innocuous individual.

Hateful Jas: Unlikeable person.

Hawspittle: Refuge for the sick and injured.

He Cud Peel An Orange In Ay's Pocket: Not great at sharing; mean spirited.

He Wudn't Giv Ye A Lift If Ye Wur In A Coffin: Not very helpful or generous.

He Wudn't Giv Ye A Scare If He Wuz A Ghost: Tight with money.

He Wudn't Giv Ye The Itch If Ay Had Two Doses Of It: An inconsiderate or stingy person.

He Wudn't Spend Xmas: He's not renowned for his generosity nor over-extravagant with his money.

He'd Git Drunk On The Smell Of A Barman's Iprin/Suckin' Brandy Balls: His capacity for holding drink is suspect.

He'd Steal The Eye Outta Yur Head An' Tell Ye Ye Wur Better Lukin' Wi'out It: He's a thief (and a liar!).

He/She Didn't Git That Behine A Stone: Sneering comment that child has inherited negative traits of one of its parents.

Head The Ball: Affectionate title for friend prone to puzzling behaviour.

Head The Grittin': Aggressive person given to wildly excessive acts.

Headbin/Headkis: Person of unpredictable disposition.

Header: Slightly unbalanced person with a tendency to act illogically.

Headin': Leaving; going off.

Heart Lik A Swingin' Breek: Unfeeling; emotionally cold.

Heavy Fut: Sound of a big man walking.

Heeds 'N' Thras: All mixed up; bits and pieces.

Heel: Bottom or last slice of bread.

Heevy: Helping hand up over a fence or other obstacle.

Heinz: Mongrel dog.

Heller Kissy: Heather Casey.

Hench: Hip bone.

Here's Me: This is what I did/said.

Here's Me An' Who's Lik May? Sarcasm directed towards person full of self-importance.

Hi, Good Lookin' – Not You, Hatchet Fis: Compliment and insult combined (usually a joke).

Hi, Git The Hair Outta Yur Eyes: Unkindly remark to bald headed footballer when he misses the ball.

Hi: Much used but meaningless ending to most Derry speech. Exclamation with the intent of attracting someone's attention.

Hingin': Suspended above the ground.

Hink: Peruse mentally.

Hippins: Nappies.

Hippiny/Make: Halfpenny in 'old' money.

Hisn't A Baldy: Clueless as to what's happening; stupid.

Hit: It.

Hiv A Bitta Sense, Wull Ye: Patronising plea to antagonist (usually the worse for drink) who's determined to have a good fight.

Hiv A Done Anyhing On Ye? Why do you dislike me so much?

Hiv A Notion A: Take a fancy to (usually) a girl/boy.

Hiv A Titter A Wit: Have some sense; behave correctly.

Hiv I Anyhing On May Belongin' Ti Ye? Sarky comment when a person catches someone else staring at them.

Hiv On: Play a joke on; playfully deceive.

Hiv Up: Legally bring to court over personal slander or other misdeed.

Hiv Ye A Big Stick There? Request from agitated mother to friend when child misbehaves, hoping that child will take it as a threat.

Hiv Ye No Gumshun? You're stupid.

Hiv Yur Eye Wiped: Have the object of your affections stolen from under your nose.

Hivin' All Yur Orders: Pampered; spoiled.

Hivn't Got Thur Sarras Ti Seek: Having their fair share of trouble.

Hoachin': Filled with, as in 'river hoachin' with fish'; smelly or dirty.

Hock: Forced to carry something (or drag it along) against one's will.

Hocklin': Coughing; trying to clear chest or throat.

Hog Nail Boots: Heavy leather footwear.

Hoke: A blow with the elbow; dig around in search of something.

Holly Eve: Hallowe'en.

Hoosh A Wee Balo: Derry lullaby.

Hope It Chokes Ye: Exclamation of resentment at not being offered share of goodies.

Horted: In pain; injured.

Houl: Hold on to.

Houl Out On: Withhold something from friends that they consider should be evenly shared.

Houl Yur Tongue/Och, Dear Aye: I agree totally; it goes without saying.

Houl Yur Whisht: Shut up!

How Wud Ye Lik Yur Head In Yur Han'? I may have to resort to violence to resolve this problem.

How Ye, Burke? Nothing doing?

How'd Ye Lik A Fat Lip? I'm getting very annoyed at you so I may contemplate a physical attack.

How're Ye Fixed, Mucker? Solicitous inquiry about a person's financial status with a view to requesting a temporary loan.

How's It Cuttin'/Goin': Friendly, inquisitive greeting.

How's The Form, Kid? Are you well? How are you today?

How's The Man? Warm greeting, usually by citizens on the periphery of city ie Drumahoe, Tullyally, etc.

Huffy Snotter: Someone who's prone to sulking.

OLD DERRY CHARACTERS

Chalk 'N' Watter: Allegedly sold water and chalk as milk from a cart.

Danny McDaid: Fanatical Derry City supporter who used to turn his back and shuffle his feet when Derry were under pressure.

Danny Wan Eye And Rosie: Could be seen any Saturday night 'fighting the bit out' and lived in old Springtown Camp.

Gacka Wacka: Victim of over-fondness for alcohol.

Gleek At The Moon: Had some neck ailment, so appeared to be permanently looking at the sky.

Hawker Lynch: Edward J Lynch was a familiar sight on the streets of the city with his sandwich board covered in advertisements, and at soccer matches, where he sold raffle tickets.

Johnny Cutthims: Drooled a little and sold the Evening Press.

Johnny The German: Former resident of the Wells area, origin of name uncertain.

Maggie McCay: Always dressed in black shawl and dark clothes; reputedly (but doubtfully) a witch.

Micky Hallstand: Came from the Lone Moor Road area. Got his name because his coat always appeared to be half hanging off him.

Slabbery Mickey: Little man who gathered rags and jampots. Drooled somewhat, hence the name.

Smokey Rogers: Came from Ferguson's Lane and had a voice like a foghorn, though most of what he said was difficult to comprehend.

Stephen: Eccentric character known to do odd things (eg carry a lorry chassis on his old bike).

Tipperary: A great street entertainer and friendly individual who unfortunately fell victim to drink and died relatively young.

Wabbits: Character who hung around the quay, pushing a bike laden down with scrap and bits and pieces.

Walk-A-Bike: Charles George O'Brien, an eccentric solicitor who never went anywhere without a bicycle but never actually rode on it.

I

I Believe Ye Where Thousands Wudn't: I don't believe you.

I Cud Laugh At You: You're behaviour shows a degree of inconsistency; why don't you practise what you preach.

I Don't Boil May Cabbage Twice: I don't repeat myself.

I Don't Know Mesel The Day: Something good has happened; I feel better than I did yesterday.

I Ee Yup? Have you risen out of bed yet?

I Hivn't The Nails Ti Scratch Mesel: I have no money to do anything.

I Luked At Better An' Niver Wuz Checked: Angry riposte to 'What are you looking at?'

I Nearly Died: I was very embarrassed/shocked.

I Wuz In Wi' May Leg: Reason for a spell in hospital.

I Wuzn't Rared On That, Ye Know: Indignant retort by someone who's just been reminded that they've neglected to pay a paltry sum of money owed.

I'll Bust Yur Clock: I'll strike you in the face.

I'll Buy Ye A Rattly: Don't be so childish.

I'll Giv Ye A Shout: I'll call for you later.

I'll Spit In Yur Eye: I detest you.

I'll Stick The Nut In Ye: I'll head butt you.

I'm As Glad: Expression of delight, usually at another's misfortune.

I'm Gaspin' Fur A Reek: I'd love a cigarette.

I'm Oney Keepin' Ye Goin': I'm only jesting with you.

I'm Sure I Wull: I will not.

I've A Hannle On May Jug: I've got a Christian name, you know.

If Ye Don't Lik It, Ye Know Wat Ti Do: Like it or lump it; it's your decision.

If Ye Had An Air Ti That, Ye Cud Sing It: Would you please stop going on about the same thing.

If Ye'd All Austin's On Ye, Ye'd Still Luk The Same: Your dress sense is questionable.

If Ye'd Anyhing In Ye: Remark questioning another's integrity or courage.

Immeejitly: At once; right away.

Impurvisin': Using unorthodox methods; making the best of what you've got.

In A Wile Stitt: Very distressed; in a terrible mess.

In Bad Twust: Not in a good mood; depressed.

In Bunch: Sharing the spoils equally.

In Debt An' Danger: In the middle of a financial crisis.

In Ernie: For real; seriously intent upon the matter at hand.

In Wi' A Shout: Having a reasonable chance of success.

Indeed Ah Wull Not: No way, José.

Inglin: Large country across the Irish Sea with London as its capital.

Injin: Front part of train; main component of car.

Iprin: Light garment worn to protect clothes when washing dishes etc.

Iss: Highest card in suit.

Istitt: Large area of council houses (eg Creggan Istitt).

It Jist Shows Ye: You see, you can never be too sure.

It Tiks Wan Ti Know Wan: Your reputation is suspect as well.

It Won't Bay Long Ti The Mornin', Sure: Don't worry, everything will be all right.

It Wud Cut Ye/Skin Ye: It's very cold.

It Wud Fit Ye Better: Another course of action would be more beneficial all round.

It Wud Melt Ye: It's very warm.

It Wuz Liftin' Lumps Outta The Road: The precipitation was intense.

It'll Do Ye Rightly: It doesn't matter that you don't want it, you're getting it anyway.

It'll Turn Ti A Pig's Fut: Unsympathetic response to anyone who complains of a minor injury or illness.

It's A Fit Day Fur Neller Man Nur Biste: That's the weather for staying indoors.

It's A Good Dose A Epsom's Ye Want: You are not really as sick as you claim.

It's A Pity A Ye: It serves you right.

It's All In The Way Ye Houl Yur Mouth: Easy, isn't it?

It's Comin' Up On The Nixt Boat: There's nothing for you.

It's Dryin' Up Fur Snow: Warning that inclement weather is on the way.

It's Dyed Aff Er Head: I suspect that that's not her hair's natural colour.

It's Early In The Day Yit: It's too soon to come to any conclusion and besides, I haven't a clue.

It's Lik A Bottle: The road is very slippery due to snow or ice.

It's Lik Tryin' Ti Fine Holy Watter In An Orange Lodge: Extremely hard to come by.

It's No Odds: It doesn't matter.

It's Well Seen: It's very obvious.

Iz My Fis Red? Sarcastic answer when someone enquires as to the whereabouts of somebody or something.

Iz That A Threat Ur A Promise? Teasing banter between sexes with suggestive undertones.

Iz That Hard Ti Sing Fur It's Hard Ti Lissin Ti? You aren't exactly Pavarotti, are you?

Iz That The Nixt Ay It? I can't take any more of this, it's just one thing after another.

Iz The Skin Of Yur Head Tight? What do you take me for?

Iz Thur Wan At Ye? Why are you scratching so much?

Iz Yur Arm Broke Ur Wat? I think it's your round.

Iz Yur Leg Broke Ur Wat? Do it yourself.

J

Ja'bone: Bone structure supporting the mouth.

Jack-An-Ory: Scornful statement of disbelief.

Jaggy: Having rough pointed edges.

Jammy: Lucky.

Jandies: Jaundice; state of revulsion.

Januwurry: First month of the year.

Jawbox: Old-style enamel sink.

Jeer: Unmentionable part of the human anatomy not too far from the tail bone.

Jeemidy God! Exclamation of disbelief/exasperation.

Jesus Wept: Exclamation of exasperation.

Jibblin': Splashing around with water.

Jist Fur Badness: Weak excuse for something being done in spite of another's objections.

Jist Wanna Thim: Only one.

Jist: Usual answer to the question 'Why?', when no justification can be found.

Joe Soap (Who Do You Hink I Am)? Fictitious alias; do you take me for a fool?

John Shumes: Former prominent Derry SDLP politician and MEP.

Join: Scold or reprimand.

Joke Wi' A Jag In It: Getting a personal rebuke across by dressing it up as comedy.

Jook: A quick look.

Jook The Beetle: One to be watched.

Jube On: Become aware of what's happening.

Juke Down: Protect oneself from danger by dropping to one's knees.

Jumpin'/Ragin': Very angry; upset.

Jurkin: Short light jacket with zipper at front.

Jute Box: Record-playing machine.

K

Keek: Blow with foot.

Keekin' An' Flingin': Lashing out wildly with arms and legs.

Keep A Wee Eye On/Out: Look after; watch out for.

Keep Goin' Ti The Meetins/Tikin' The Tablets: You're talking rubbish; frustration is setting in.

Keepin' Dick: Acting as lookout during secretive undertaking.

Kilt: Severely reprimanded; killed.

Kine A Haff Middlin': Just average; mediocre.

Kinnlin': The basic essentials for making a fire (eg sticks, paper, etc).

Kip: Establishment of dubious reputation; a light sleep.

Kipp: Piece of clothing resembling a cloak; piece of land jutting out into sea (eg Kipp of Good Hope).

Kipper: Trick or practical joke.

Kiss It Up Ti God: Advice given by one child to another before eating a sweet they've just scraped off the ground.

Kissin' The Altar Rails: What a person perceived to be a hypocrite does every Sunday, while sinning the rest of the week.

Kittlin: Young pussy cat.

Knack A The Mug: Dexterity at playing marbles.

Knock Yur Pan Out: Toil long and hard for little or no reward.

Know Wat's Stickin' Ti Ye: Be painfully aware of someone's retribution.

Knuspipper: Printed communication used by the media to inform the public of interesting events.

Knyam: Cry, bemoan or complain unduly.

Knyuck: Steal.

Kuge: Extremely large; of massive proportions.

Kugo/Shugo Kwun: Hugo Quinn.

Kwuns: Five children born of the same mother at the same time.

L

Ladies And Gentlemen And Baldy-Headed Countrymen: Shakespearian parody designed to attract the attention of anyone who'll listen.

Land In: Arrive on an unexpected visit, one which is perhaps not one hundred per cent appreciated.

Landed: In a promising position for further success.

Lantrin: Portable means of illumination; small lamp.

Latch On Ti: Form unwelcome alliance with.

Latchico: Undesirable character; hanger-on.

Laughin' An' Keh-heyin': Sniggering and muttering in a very annoying manner.

Laughin': Doing well; on the path to success.

Lave: Depart; go away.

Laverty: Place to do one's ablutions.

Lay Ar Faller: The Lord's Prayer.

Lay Go: Release me; unhand me at once.

Layin' Wide Ti The World: Door left open and unattended.

Least A May Notion: Last thing on my mind.

Leenge: Make swinging blow at; jump at.

Left Lik A Kiltie: Left standing alone and embarrassed.

Leggered: Covered in dirt, muck or other unsightly substances.

Leller: The outer skin of a range of bovine creatures used to adorn the body when treated.

Leller In Ti: Attack with vigour and gusto.

Lepercorn: Mythical Irish dwarf dressed in colourful clothes.

Lessa That An' More A The Oller: Jovial resistance to cuddle by member of the opposite sex.

Lessa Yur Oul Buck: Don't be so cheeky now.

Let A Roar At: Shout at in an attempt to modify someone's behaviour.

Lettin' On: Pretending to tell the truth.

Level: Knock someone to the ground.

Libber Pardy: British political party with socialist origins.

Libberarchie: Flamboyant American singer and pianist (deceased).

Libberer: Person who toils on building site or does other manual work.

Libery: Place where you go to borrow books and study.

Lidder On: After a while; sometime in the near future.

Lie Down An' Die Right: I couldn't care less if you're sick.

Lift Yur Feet: Hurry up.

Lift Yur Han' Ti: Make threatening gesture towards, or actually strike, someone.

Lifted: Arrested, usually in the middle of the night.

Lik A Dog's Hine Leg: In a very untidy and disordered condition.

Lik A Duntin' Bull: In a foul, bad-tempered frame of mind.

Lik A Feller: Extremely light; weighing hardly anything.

Lik A Fibre Mattress: Unkind description of person with coarse and unkempt red hair.

Lik A Hen Lukin' Ore A Whitewashed Wall: Description of someone (usually wearing glasses) peering from behind something.

Lik A Rake: Very thin; lightly built.

Lik A Week's Work: Difficult, arduous task.

Lik A Wet Dishcloth: Looking tired and jaded.

Lick An' A Promise: A very superficial cleaning.

Lik An Oul Woman Wi' A Straw Ass: Unable to take any rough treatment; description of very fragile individual.

Lik Death Warmed Up: A terrible sight altogether.

Lik Nellie Ramsey's: Very untidy (as of house).

Lik Nellie Sidebottom: Grossly overweight.

Lik Our Hanna: Unkempt and dirty.

Lik Shipquay Gate: Quite large or wide; of gross proportions.

Lik Soups: That's highly improbable.

Lik The Oul Woman's Stews: Unwelcome; disliked.

Lik The Scotch Boat: Sound of someone snoring or blowing their nose loudly.

Lik Two Matches Stickin' Out Ay A Spud: Unkind description of a small fat person with thin legs.

Linky Long Legs: Tall thin person.

Lipton's Orphan: Pitiful child.

Lisses: Long pieces of string used for securing boots and shoes.

Lissin, Mit: Ominous opener to further verbal, or possibly physical, conflict.

Lissinin': Taking note of what's being said; paying attention.

Liver Lips: Insensitive remark made about someone with an oversized mouth.

Livin' Ore The Brush: Cohabiting.

Livin': Infested with fleas or lice; dirty.

Lizzie Drippin': Affectionate nickname for small child.

Lock: Indefinable amount of anything.

Lodger: Small uncut loaf of bread.

Long Chinny: American horror movie actor of yesteryear.

Long Shootie: Street football game where ball is kicked from 'goal' to 'goal' with no outfield play.

Long Trams: Tall gangly person.

Long Yarn: An awful bore.

Loo Warm: Tepid.

Lorn An' Harly: Classic American comedy duo.

Losin' The Bap: Getting angry or annoyed.

Lost: Being in a position where talents aren't recognized or appreciated.

Low: Mean; underhand.

Lucky Duck: Children's description of recipient of good fortune.

Luk Over Yur Rentbook, You're Four Weeks Behine: Derry version of a line from the Eddie Fisher song 'I'm Walking Behind You'.

Luk That Wudda Cut Coul Steel: Ominous, threatening stare.

Luk Wat The Wun Blew In: Friendly greeting to someone not seen for a long time.

Luk Wat Ye Made May Do Now: I know it's my fault but I have to blame someone else.

Lukalik: A person who strongly resembles another.

Lukin' At The Style: Occupation, usually of the ladies, whereby they observe carefully what all the other girls are wearing.

Lukin' Far In Front A Ye: Being too optimistic about the future.

Lukkit The Ship A Ye: Please tidy yourself up.

Luks Lik He Lost A Bob An' Found A Tanner: A pessimistic approach to life.

Luks Lik Ye Wur Dragged Through A Hage Backwards: Of an unkempt, bedraggled appearance.

Luks More Lik 'Imself Now: Sympathetic comment usually addressed to a corpse at a wake.

Luks Odd: Seems so different; completely changed.

Lured Stiff: Delighted.

Lured: Happy; excited; pleased.

Luvly Head A Skin: Light-hearted reference to bald-headed man.

M

Ma, He's Pullin' The Arms Outta The Blankets: Standard Derry joke, said to have originated in Springtown Camp, where poor people had to use old coats as blankets.

Maisles: Contagious disorder where red spots appear on the body.

Make A Rise: Make some money, usually from gambling.

Make A Tear At: Rush at in anger.

Make A Winde At: Lash out wildly with fist.

Man Dear: Expression of jovial surprise.

Manky: Of inferior quality; second rate.

Martyr: Long-suffering individual who never receives much sympathy.

Massacray: Slaughter; complete rout.

May Gut's Hingin' Outta May: I could be doing with a fish supper.

May Han' On Yur Coat/Hat/Gansey: I think the particular item referred to is nice.

May Head's Deeved: I can't stand it anymore; fed up with something.

May Lone: On my own; by myself.

May Moller: My father's wife.

May The National Assistance Remain Always With Us: Derry 'prayer' playfully praising the virtues of government benefits.

Meejim: Not extreme on one side or another (eg meejim rare).

Melder: Terrible mess; loud chaotic mixture of sound.

Mell: Violently strike.

Mibby: Perhaps.

Midger: Determine by measuring tape or other means the dimensions of.

Midget: Minute insect whose bite causes great distress and irritation.

Mik A Mouth A Yursel: Disgrace yourself in public; act like an idiot.

Mik Up: Get back on speaking terms with; face cosmetics used by women (and sometimes men).

Mikkin' A Wile Ship At: Not being very successful; pathetic effort.

Mikkin' Fisses: Pulling facial contortions.

Mikkin' Sheep's Eyes: Fluttering the eyelids to attract the opposite sex.

Mimmy Gollagur: Mamie Gallagher.

Mind/Member? Do you recollect what I just said?

Mind Ye: Assertion of truth.

Mind Yur Big Splas: Please move your feet.

Minellium: A thousand years.

Mingin': Dirty and smelly.

Mingy: Not very generous.

Missin': Description of car not running smoothly.

Mizzlin': Raining lightly.

Mockin's Catchin': Superstitious warning not to mimic anyone in unfortunate circumstances lest a similar fate may result.

Moderin: Contemporary; up to date.

Moller A Sarras: Person who appears to carry all the troubles of the world on their shoulders.

Moller: Female parent.

Mon You: An attempt to attract someone's attention in order to get them to do something or suffer the consequences.

Monkey Glands: Insult levelled at hateful type.

Moocher: Lethargic person; a scrounger; a footballer who does little but scavenge for goals.

Mooter: Large marble.

Morbs: State of depression.

More Coats Than An Onion: Wearing too much clothing.

More Fisses Than The Guilthall Clock: Not very trustworthy; sly and deceitful.

Mortified: Totally embarrassed or disgraced.

Mouth: Person who is always boasting or bragging.

Mouthwash: Description of someone who bathes another in saliva while kissing.

Mozzy: Large stone, usually for throwing.

Mucka: Thin moustache.

Mucker: Friend or pal.

Mulk: White liquid obtained from cows and taken as a nourishing drink.

Munce: Plural of month.

Murder: Hard to bear; trouble; very difficult.

Murry Dordy: Mary Doherty.

Mussly: Of a strong, well-developed appearance.

Myin's: Belonging to me.

DIFFERENCES OF OPINION

A Bunch A Fives: A fistful of knuckles, usually administered forcefully.

Al Bust Yur Head: Threat of impending violence.

Al Dance On Ye: You're asking for trouble.

Al Do Ye: Take yourself off before I beat you up.

Al Go Thru Ye Lik A Dose A Salts: I'd advise you to leave immediately.

Al Hiv Ye, Mucker: Swords or pistols?

Al Pan Ye: I'll thump your head.

Al Spit In Yur Eye: I detest you.

Al Swing On Ye: Threat of violence from female to male.

Aye, You An' Whose Army? Derisive response to threat of attack.

Bitt The Linin' Outta: Give a severe beating to.

Bleenge: Massive swinging blow.

Bline Swipe: Wild swing with fist at some part of another's anatomy.

Brain: Inflict serious injury on someone's head with a heavy implement.

Cuttin' Up Rough: Just about to be violent.

De Ye Want Yur Head In Yur Hans? Direct challenge to opponent.

Eat: Violently take issue with.

Git Scripped: Go away; you're not on.

Go An' Tik A Runnin' Jump: Uncompromising term of refusal.

Quare Dig: Painful body blow.

Stikkit: Instant comment on being refused share of something.

The Laugh'll Bay On The Oller Side Ay Yur Fis: I would advise you to stop smirking.

Wile Keekin': A serious beating.

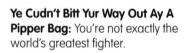

Ye Cudn't Bitt Yur Way Out Ay A Pipper Bag: You're not exactly the world's greatest fighter.

BARS AND BOOZE

A Munk Bay The Neck: A bottle of beer.

Are Ye Standin'? Broad hint to another to buy a drink.

Blarge: Large amount of drink.

Blootered: Very intoxicated.

Christian Bror: A pint of Guinness.

Futliss: Walking erratically due to excess alcohol.

Haff Cut/Tubed: On the way to drunken bliss.

Haff 'N' A Bottle: Standard Derry order in a pub.

On The Tear/Rip: An extended drinking session.

Outta Yur Mind: In an alcohol-induced world of one's own.

Pallatic: In a different universe.

Porter-Belly: Overweight through consuming too much black beer.

Scootered: The level of intoxication below 'blootered'.

Stovin: Pretty drunk.

Wee Hot Haff: A measure of whiskey and hot water.

Wee Tritt: A little drink on a special occasion.

Well-On: Three-quarters-way drunk.

N

Naaaaa: Semi-negative answer when person is not sure if they mean yes or no.

Nags: Men's personal under-garments.

Nanchin': Chewing noisily.

Narra Nan: Insult levelled at thin, mean person.

Natch: Naturally; of course.

Naw: Negative response.

Naw, Am A Liar: Hold on, I think I've made a mistake.

Naw, Am Haff Left: Quip in response to question, 'Are you all right?'

Nawhin': Nothing.

Nawhin' Strange Or Startlin'? Hello; no earth-shattering news?

Nawhin' Wud Do Ye: You had to have it your own way; you deserve it.

Nearly Tik The Han' A Ye: Accepted quickly and eagerly before opportunity is lost.

Ned The Kwa: Term applied to person who displeases another.

Neller Air Nur Smell: Devoid of musical form; tuneless.

New Light In The Wunda: Something unusual or surprising.

Newins: Out of the ordinary; a new occurrence.

Newrp: Nag or nuisance.

Nibbers: People who live in the same street or housing estate; a popular TV soap programme.

Nice Ti Yur Fis But Wud Stick A Knife In Yur Back: Treacherous; two-faced.

Nick: Put out half-smoked cigarette; to steal.

Nickie Cakes: Large plain biscuits; very easy.

Niver Dips A Han': Not overenthusiastic about doing chores or spending money.

Niver Diz A Tap: Is quite averse to anything resembling work.

Niver Nawhin': Disagreement with football referee's decision.

Niver Seen Watter: Considered to be dirty.

Nixt Durr Nibber: The person living closest to you.

Nixt Time Wur Lukin' Fur Hot Watter, We'll Send Fur Ye: Joking remark made to rejected blood donor.

No Harm Ti Ye: This will probably upset you (usually precedes an uncomplimentary remark).

No Heat That Day: It's cold today.

No Sense: Prone to illogical action.

No Toe: Nonsense nickname for friend.

None A May Notion: No intention of doing so.

Nose Lik A Bullhook: Unkind description of someone with a large curved proboscis.

Not A Bit Backward About Comin' Forward: Not very shy; outgoing.

Not A Boul In The Dresser: Totally toothless.

Not A Broken Bit: In good condition.

Not A Mute: No sound; completely quiet.

Not A Nounce: Not very sensible; naive.

Not A Pik On Ye: Underfed; skinny.

Not A Thing In: No shopping done; nothing to offer a visitor.

Not A Wane Washed: Nothing achieved, completed or carried out.

Not All There: Unbalanced; not fully in control.

Not Asked If Ye'd A Mouth On Ye: Not offered any food or drink on a visit.

Not At Yursel: Unwell; sick.

Not Fussed On: Not too keen about.

Not Haff Wise: Capable of strange behaviour.

Not In Wi': Out of favour with.

Not Interruptin' Yur Discourse: Excuse me for butting in.

Not Worth Tuppence: Taken weak or very nervous; useless.

Nuggit: Type of white soft toffee.

Nur Me Eller: You can count me out as well.

O

Obcast: Bring up past misdeeds to embarrass or compromise.

Oblege: Help out of difficulties; grant request.

Och, God Wuz Good Ti Im: Usually said of someone who has just died in agony.

Och, You're Aw Right, Sure: No, thanks.

Octaypuss: Large sea creature with eight tentacles.

Odd/Odd As Two Lefts: Disinclined to speak; moody; very eccentric.

Oddamadig: Needing minimum supervision (eg oddamadig washing machine).

Oddim: The season preceding winter.

Odds: Spare change in pocket.

Oddyince: People in the auditorium; the listeners.

On The Batter: Up and about and working hard.

On Ti A Good Thing: Discovering a lucrative line of business (usually by chance).

Oney: Only.

Open: Inflict injury on someone's head.

Optober: The tenth month of the year.

Ord'nray: Run-of-the-mill; mundane.

Orfant: Parentless child alone in the world.

Ornament: Derisory term for person of dull personality.

Orr Ite, Mucker? How are you today, my friend?

Oul Blow: Person who embellishes story; windbag.

Oul Boot: Severely ugly person.

Oul Crack: Unacceptable talk or behaviour.

Oul Fashioned: Devious; sly; set in one's ways.

Oul Granny Grunt: Reference to a child too advanced for its years.

Oul Hardie Hole: Nickname for stingy person.

Oul Heiffer: Insulting name for female.

Oul Lick: Someone who tries to curry favour with another.

Oul Lilt A Da: Unwelcome character; bore.

Oul Poser: Person showing off as if they were someone of note, style or celebrity.

Oul Relic: Unwelcome, boring type of person.

Oul Rip: Gossiping woman; trouble maker.

Oul Sickener: Bore; distasteful character.

Oul Slippy Tit: One who gets away with 'murder'; jammy individual.

Oul Stickin' Plaster: Hanger-on; unwanted companion.

Oul Wormy: Most unpleasant name for weak, disliked person.

Over The Ways: Vague directional advice.

Oxter: Armpit.

CHILDHOOD DELICACIES

In the heady days before Harry Potter and Angry Birds inhabited the digital universe, children of all ages took their few 'old' pence pocket money to the corner shop to treat themselves. Available there was a small but exciting selection of down-to-earth 'swiddies' which always tasted great and seemed to last all day. Such were the days of innocence and simplicity, expectation and hope, and childhood delicacies. How many can you remember?

Aniseed Balls	Everlasting Strip	Lucky Dips
Banana Splits	Fizz	Peggy's Leg
Bazookas	Flying Saucers	Penny Dainties
Black Jacks	Gobstoppers	Pineapple Chunks
Brandy Balls	Goldmines	Puff Candy
Broken Biscuits	Hippiny Chix	Spangles
Bubbley Gum	Jube Jubes	Swiddie Fags
Carmels	Liquorice Pipes	Swiddie Tobacco
Chewing Gum Balls	Liquorice Sticks	Toffee Apples
Danny Boys	Love Hearts	Whoppers
	Lucky Bags	

MARLEY RULES

Bendy Knocks: I can hit opponent's marble to restart game if a third person has gained an advantage.

Drops: You have to drop your marble on mine from shoulder height with your eyes closed.

High Drops/Heights: You must drop your marble on mine from as high a position as possible.

High Scoots: You have to scoot your marble down on mine from a great height.

Ivryhing An' Nawhin': I can do what I like, but you have to wait a turn.

Layin': I don't have to throw my marble up to the mug (hole) if I don't want to.

Long Scoots: You have to scoot your marble at mine from a great distance off.

Mug: Hole into which marble is directed.

Mugs: I can throw my marble into the hole.

No Dibs: You're not allowed to hit my marble.

No Reddins: I can put whatever I like in front of my marble so you can't hit it.

Reddins: I'm allowed to clear away all obstacles in order to get a better shot at your marble.

Scoots: You have to propel your marble rapidly with your thumb against your finger.

Skees On: I'm allowed to strike an opponent's marble and use it to hit another person's marble.

Squarins: I can move around in a circular motion to get a better shot at your marble.

P

Paddles: Footrests on bicycle used as means of propulsion.

Pallatic: Intoxicated to the point of immobility.

Pamp: Sound car horn.

Pantamine: Yuletide stage extravaganza; a laughable situation.

Pantwatchin': Spying on courting couples.

Parly: Neutral zone in children's game of 'Tig'.

Pass No Remark: Ignore; don't take any notice.

Pass Yursel: Give reasonable account; not disgrace yourself.

Patsy Quinn: Former French Derry City football star, Pascal Vaudequin.

Pee The Bed: Dandelion.

Peeana: Large musical instrument with black and white keys.

Peeky: Pale looking; appearing unwell.

Peg: Throw.

Peggin' Breeks: Throwing stones.

Petted Lip: On the verge of tears; huffing.

Pewmooney: Disease of the lungs.

Physic: Laxative.

Pick The Bones Outta That: Said by someone who's just spat on the ground.

Pickin' An' Dabbin': Not exactly eating meals voraciously.

Piece: Slice of bread; a sandwich.

Pig Ignernt: Very rude or bad mannered.

Piggin': Very dirty (as of house).

Pignose: Unkindly reference to part of another's anatomy.

Pihnt: Coloured liquid used for decorating walls etc.

Pillakiss: Cover for bed cushion.

Pinnickity: Extremely fussy; annoyingly meticulous about detail.

Piss: Rate or velocity.

Pist: Sticky gel-like substance used for hanging wallpaper.

Pistrey: Assorted sweet buns.

Pitchur A Misery: Of a somewhat crestfallen appearance.

Plague: Person intensely disliked.

Plagued: Repeatedly pestered or annoyed.

Plank: Hide or stash away for later.

Plank Yursel Down: Occupy a place where you're not entirely welcome.

Pleece: Law officers.

Plett: Long tail of interwoven hair on head.

Plits: Pieces of round porcelain for eating dinner off.

Plowter: Plod through mud; trudge along.

Plumpin': Boiling vigorously; raining heavily.

Poke Man: Ice-cream vendor operating from a van.

Polar Neck: Type of jumper that goes right up to the chin.

Pooch: Small leather money bag; gun holster.

Poor Wee Bit Ay A Wane: A young person who is being maltreated.

Poreshon: An amount or piece of (eg a poreshon of chips).

Pounded: Out of breath; exhausted.

Poundies: Mixture of mashed potatoes, scallions and butter.

Poyshin: Toxic substance; a terrible taste.

Prattie Fadge: Potato bread.

Probbly: In all likelihood.

Prodisin: Non-Catholic.

Prog: Steal apples from an orchard.

Propergander: Lies put out by governments in times of conflict or war.

Puck: Chosen; selected.

Puddin': Someone not very good at football; generally useless person.

Puddy: Plaster-like substance for securing pane of glass in window frame.

Puke: Unsavoury character; to throw up.

Pull A Flanker: Carry off a neat con trick; fool everybody.

Pull On Ye/Stick On Ye: Get dressed in a hurry.

Pulled Up: Confronted by a demand to explain past indiscretions.

Pullin' An' Haulin': Treating roughly; manhandling.

Punchur: Unwanted aperture which causes tyre to deflate.

Punchy: Dense; not in command of ones senses.

Punkawalla: Affectionate nickname for friend.

Purscripshun: Note from doctor permitting patient to obtain medicine or pills from chemist.

Put A Bush In Thon Gap: Request to close the door on exiting the premises.

Put A Han' On: Make physical contact in order to cause bodily harm.

Put In Ageenst Ye: Speaking ill of someone to cause them trouble.

Put The Blah On: Curse; bring bad luck upon.

Put The Wunda In: Break the window.

Put Ye Aff Yur Notion: Make you change your mind.

Put Ye In Minda: Make you think of; remind you of.

Q-R

Quare 'N' Saft: Not at all queer or soft; not to be believed.

Quare Colour: Having a good suntan.

Quare Form: In good spirits; happy.

Quare Gunk: Bitter shock or disappointment.

Quare Han' At: Good at the job; dexterous.

Quare Packin': Good food; filling meal.

Queeng: Female monarch.

Quet It: Stop now; give it up; desist.

Quzz: Event where chairperson asks questions on various subjects and panel or audience answer.

Qwud: One pound sterling.

Ramscootrify: Completely destroy (usually applied to a person).

Randi Boo: Noisy gathering; mêlée.

Rare Boy/Duck: A strange person who acts erratically.

Rasslin': Type of close contact sport akin to judo.

Raycord: Circular wax or vinyl recording of music or speech.

Razure: Instrument for shaving hair off face and other parts of the body.

Reach Fur: Physically attack.

Ready Fur The Hills: At wits' end; approaching breaking point.

Ready Fur The Ragbag: Description of clothes (usually still worn) that have seen better days.

Ready Ti Squeal: Unable to take anymore.

Real Derry: Having a pronounced Derry accent.

Real Dose: Insufferable person; pest.

Redner: Blushing; highly embarrassed.

Redd: Clean up; tidy away.

Reel: Idiot; fool.

Rench: Rinse with water.

Ressliss: Fidgety; unable to relax.

Rickety Wheel: Circular spinning contraption used as a means of gambling at funfair.

Rickle A Bones: Thin frail person.

Riddly Gun: Automatic weapon.

Rift: Bring up gas from stomach.

Right Oul Haff: Attractive female.

Right Oul Screw: Substantial sum of money.

Ringin'/Seepin': Soaking wet.

Rinnin': Precipitation.

Rise A Whole Stink: Create a serious fuss or disturbance.

Rissin': Running in competition against others; moving fast.

Roarin' Outta Im: Shouting at the top of his voice.

Rooked: Left without money; usually as a result of gambling.

Rotton Wi' Dough: Affluent; well-to-do.

Roulin': Moving along the ground in the manner of a wheel.

Royit: Civil disturbance.

Rubber Dinky: Small inflatable boat.

Rubbitch: Waste collected by the bin man; stupid talk.

Ructions: Uproar; general mêlée.

Ruin The Coops: Spoil everything for everybody.

Ruinated: Completely spoiled or destroyed.

Ruined/Spoilt Rotten: Very spoiled/pampered (as of a child).

Rumberella: Device for deflecting rain.

Run Away Wi' Yursel: Go off at a tangent; get confused.

Run In Ti: Meet up with; encounter.

Runnin' About Lik A Yo-yo: In a tizzy; searching frantically.

Runnin' Roun' Lik Sumfin' Not Wise: Mental condition giving cause for concern.

Runnin' Ti The Doctors Wi' Yur Ears: Badly in need of having your ears syringed or suffering from some other auditory problem.

Rushie: Frenetic form of street football for kids.

FOOTBALL FLAK

Av A Wane In The House Who Cud Keek A Ball Harder: Comment on half-hearted play.

Ay Cudn't Save Ciggies: Gordon Banks he's not.

Big Git: Large attendance at a match.

Blarge: To administer a hefty uncultured kick of the ball, more in hope than intent.

C'mon, Badgerovitch: Overheard at Derry City v Red Star Belgrade game.

C'mon, Derry, Skin Them: Supporters' rallying call.

Dig A Hole: Unsympathetic remark shouted when member of opposing team is injured.

Don't Send Im Aff, Ref, He's The Best Man We've Got: Subtle criticism of whole team effort.

Giv That Ref A Blue/Green/Red Etc Jersey: Accusation of bias against match official.

Hi, Hiv Ye A Hole In Yur Fut Ur Wat? That wasn't a very accurate pass.

Hi, Ref, De Ye Wan A Lenna May Glasses? That was definitely a misjudgement on behalf of the official.

Hi, Ref, Did Ye Swally Yur Wussle Ur Wat? Why didn't you detect that foul play?

His Laces Must Be Tied Tigether Or Sumfin': Said about unco-ordinated player.

Houl On Ti It, It'll Be A Better Match Wi'out It: Remark passed when ball is kicked into the crowd.

May Granny Cudda Saved That Wan An' She's Oney Got Wan Arm: Somewhat unkind comment made about an incompetent goalie.

Movin' Stychays: Sarcastic reference to inactive Derry City players.

No Wonder Ye Spend Most Of Yur Time On The Bench: You're little asset to the team.

Shower A Slabbers: Unfortunate Derry opposition.

Wipe-O: Encouragement from fans to player to adopt unsavoury tactics.

Ye Cudn't Catch A Coul: Why do you keep dropping the ball?

Ye Cudn't Cross Yur Legs: Judgement made on poor passer.

Ye Cudn't Pick Yur Nose: I disagree with your (the manager's) choice of players.

Ye Cudn't Run A Message: Incisive judgement made on slow player.

Food and Drink

A Drop A Tay: Light hot refreshment.

Baps: Tasty round buns, nice with butter.

Brackfist: First meal in the morning.

Brocken: Porridge oats.

Chesterbred: Thick square bun made from dubious ingredients (also known as a sinker).

Chookie: Chicken.

Crips: Multi-flavoured fried potato slices.

Cuttin' Loaf: Yesterday's bread, bought when times were hard.

Ditts: Exotic fruit from the East.

Hern: Salty fish containing thousands of bones.

Injin Mail: Type of reddish-coloured porridge oats.

Lemmanade: Mixture of water, sugar and gas with a variety of flavours.

Lofa Brown: One unit of wheaten bread.

Swuss Roll: Rolled-up spongy pastry filled with jam.

Tamada: Red seedy fruit used in salads and sandwiches.

Turnover: Diamond-shaped bun with blob of jam in the middle.

Wiffer: Two thin rectangular biscuits with ice-cream in between them.

S

Saft Ca: Do you really think I believe what you're saying?

Saft Mark: Person easily deceived or taken in.

Saftee, Are Ye Chew' A Breek? You're not so stupid.

Sail In: Appear suddenly, usually uninvited.

Sanitry Man: Person who periodically calls to make sure your lavatory is clean.

Santy: Father Christmas.

Say Black, Ye'll Niver Git That Back: Said by children at the conclusion of a successful business transaction.

Say Boo: Some Derry singers' interpretation of a line in the Jim Reeves song 'Anna Marie' (C'est vous).

Scaldie: Young, featherless bird.

Scalp: Sharp slap (usually administered to unruly child).

Scandal: Gossip; news.

Scar: Shock or fright.

Scobe: Eat with gusto.

Scobie: Turnip.

Scoodle: Nip off in a hurry to do a little errand.

Scootie Hole: Gap in hedge or fence.

Score: The act of attracting a member of the opposite sex.

Scorrick: Odds and ends in a pocket; the last dregs of a cigarette.

Scotchie: Type of scout's lift using the hands to help a friend over a wall.

Scraggly: Very untidily dressed; unkempt.

Scrake A Dawn: First light.

Scran: Small amount of money (or possessions) gained by dubious means; the scant remains of anything.

Scratcher: Bed.

Screenge: Search frantically for money or other essentials.

Scrillions: Very large number, precise value unknown.

Scrinkly: Describes the sound of tinfoil.

Scrippin': Scratching sound.

Scrippins: Leftovers; dregs.

Scrunch: Squash; crunch.

Scuse Me Fur Breathin': Sorry I opened my mouth.

See If Ye Brak Yur Leg, Al Brak Yur Oller Wan: Sadistic warning given by concerned parent to child who persists in indulging in playful but dangerous activities.

See Ye After: Cheerio.

Seezy: It's easy.

Sellatipp: Sticky tape used for securing parcels etc.

Sendnil: Weekly Derry newspaper.

Sent Fur (I Thought I Wuz): Dead.

Serpent: Devious, untrustworthy type.

Set Fut In: Visit someplace after a long absence.

Set: On the road to success.

Settle Yur Head: Relax; take it easy.

Shadda: Dark image cast by person or object blocking off light.

Shade: Small building in the back yard used for storing materials or working in.

Shake Han's, Bror, You're A Rogue An' Am Anoller: Friendly greeting from adult to child.

She Cud Liv' Aff The Smell Ay An Oily Rag: She's a very thrifty lady.

She Hinks She Is Sumfin': She has big ideas about herself; a would-be snob.

She's More Pihnt On Er Than Wat's In Carlin's: She wears far too much make-up.

Sheely Wi' The Wee Girls: Boys should be boys.

Shift: Type of nightshirt.

Shintalla: Large housing estate, north of Derry city centre.

Ship: Type of unsliced loaf.

Shipquay Street's A Slippy Street Ti Slide Upon: Dangerous Derry tongue twister.

Shipway Pliss: Pedestrianised area in front of Derry's historic Guildhall.

Shooey Swinny: Hugh Sweeney.

Shoogly Shoo: Type of swing in children's playground.

Shootie In: Football game in which everybody has a free shot at the nets.

Showlders Lik An Olive Oil Bockle: Of slight build; skinny.

Shot Down: A loser in love.

Show Up: Completely humiliate in public.

Shugger: Crystals of either cane or beet used for sweetening tea or in the making of confectionery.

Shuman Beins: People; Homo sapiens.

Shut Yur Big Yappin' Mouth, Wud Ye: For God's sake, give it a rest.

Siff: Secure from harm; lockable metal container for storing money and other valuables.

Siff's A Row A Houses In Fahan Street: Extremely unsafe; about to fall down.

Siller: Seagoing member of the armed forces.

Silly Bugle: Person who does something stupid.

Simmit: A vest.

Singil: One unit; unmarried person.

Sint: Deceased person who has been canonised by the Church; goody type.

Sit At Peace: Command to child to desist from annoying activity.

Sittin' In The Middle A May Dinner: In the process of eating lunch.

Sittin' Wi' A Fis On: Looking bad-tempered or depressed.

Sittin' Wittin': Hanging about in an impatient and irritated frame of mind.

Six Months: What you get when you feel you're talking to yourself.

Siz Who? Inquiry as to where recently communicated information came from.

Sk'boo: Convenient alias when reluctant to give real name.

Skahy: Messy meal of unusual ingredients.

Skelligan/Skellington: The bony framework of the body.

Skelly: Cross-eyed.

Skelp/Skite: Sharp slap.

Skip It An' Play Gulf: Never mind, forget it.

Skittery: Small in size or number.

Skitts: Equipment that can be attached to the feet for purposes of either sport or recreation, and can be either 'ice' or 'roller'.

Skive Off: Sneak away without doing fair share of the chores.

Skivin': Feigning illness or using excuse in order to avoid doing work; malingering.

Skunnered: Greatly dispirited; totally fed up.

Slabber: Loudmouth; unlikeable person.

Slabbers: Saliva drooling from mouth.

Slag: To make disparaging comments about someone.

Sleekid: Sly; devious; dishonest.

Slingy: Primitive weapon made from Y-shaped branch and length of rubber, used to propel missiles through the air.

Slip Off, Nobody's Lukin': Advice given by fans to footballer who's not having a very good game.

Slip The Backs: Get away; get off lightly.

Slit: Rectangular tile used in roofing houses etc.

Slup Up Yur Sloup There's More In The Slaucepan: A little nonsense doggerel to encourage children to eat.

Smidgin: A small amount.

Smittle: Contagious.

Smoller: Suffocate by means of placing something over the mouth.

Snoodle: Sidle up craftily to someone with the intention of gaining their favours.

Snotterbox: Nose.

So Am Are: I certainly am.

Sola: A card game for one.

Sore Dose: Hard to stick; unlikeable person.

Sore Han': Large piece of bread with butter and jam.

Sore Head: Type of plain pastry.

Sore On Ye: Sympathetic remark when one is treated badly or unjustly.

Soun: Just fine; perfect; dependable; trustworthy.

Soun Affair: Good idea; expression of agreement.

Soun Filla: Good, decent, upstanding sort of individual.

Soun Job: Satisfactory outcome for all concerned.

Sowl Out: Nothing left to sell.

Speel: To climb up.

Spisser: One who is perpetually in a world of his own.

Spiss Kadett: One undergoing training to be a 'spisser'.

Spit Out Or Ye'll Grow Horns: Advice given to children after they've bumped heads.

Spittin': Beginning to rain.

Spla-Futted: Having flat, broad feet positioned at a wide angle to each other.

Split: To open a wound in someone's head.

Spoil The Meetin': Throw a spanner in the works; interrupt current plans.

Sprasie: Sixpence in 'old' money.

Square Up: Pay outstanding monies owed.

Stacks: Lots of; plenty.

Stacks A Wans: A very big crowd.

Stan' At Peace, Wull Ye: Will you please stop moving about.

Stan' In: Take shelter from the rain.

Standin' Lik A Lilty: Looking very silly and embarrassed.

Standin' Gawkin': Staring with mouth open and blank look on face.

Standin' Wi' Yur Two Arms The Wan Length: Looking stupid and out of place.

Start (Someone): Provoke a person to fight.

Starvin': Very cold or hungry.

Stews, Farts An' Onions: Answer given by parent to child in reply to 'What's for dinner?'

Stews: Food in general – mince, potatoes, onions and carrots in particular.

Stibble: Building where horses are fed and sheltered.

Stick: Stand or tolerate.

Stickin' Out: Wonderful; great.

Stikkit: Acrimonious grunt when refused share of something.

Still Shukin' About: Getting around reasonably well.

Stinkin' Wi' Hunger An' Fartin' Wi' Pride: Reluctant to admit that you're poor.

Stittmint: Unwelcome letter from bank giving details of one's financial status.

Stocious/Stovin: Highly intoxicated.

Stop It Ah Luv It: Jovial resistance to cuddling.

Stoul: Taken without owner's consent.

Strainey: Small round object that tricksters try to pass off as genuine marble.

Strenth: Measure of one's physical capabilities.

Strik' May Stiff Stone Dead: I'm definitely not telling lies.

Stroop: Spout of kettle or teapot.

Stumor: Person whose strongest trait is his stupidity.

Stump: Core or remains of half-eaten apple.

Stychay: Likeness of person carved in stone.

Suck The Butts: Person who tries to get as many puffs as possible from a cigarette.

Sumfin': Generic term for matter.

Sure All Belongin' Ti Ye Wuz No Good: I have doubts about your family's integrity.

Surra Mourne: Sarah Moran.

Suss: Right, we're all set.

Swalla: Swift flying birds whose appearance is reputed to herald the beginning of summer.

Swally: A good drink.

Swappin' Spittles: Kissing.

Sweel: Wind round and round.

Sweem: Propel oneself through water using the arms and legs.

Swiddies: Confectionery of all sorts.

Swing Fur: Be so enraged as to attempt violence.

Swipe: Take something that does not belong to you.

Swizz: Playfully spinning a child round and round very quickly.

Swundle: Blatantly cheat out of money or other possessions.

Symmetry: Place to bury the dead.

T

Tackle: Attempt to smooth talk a girl; query a past indiscretion.

Talent: Available girls sought by eager boys or vice versa.

Talk Ti May, Wud Ye: Female's request to friend when trying to hide from some unwelcome would-be suitor.

Tank: Sum total of all money owned (and about to be squandered).

Tanked Up: Highly intoxicated and in a very volatile frame of mind.

Tant: Tempt or taunt.

Tanted: Rotten (as of fruit).

Tap Up: Ask to leave a girl or boy home.

Tap: Beg or borrow money.

Tartar: Unattractive name for rough, argumentative female; malevolent woman.

Tartles: Raggedy clothes; knots in hair.

Tarts: Various types of pastry.

Tatched: Connected to (eg the bike was tatched to the railings).

Tay: An addictive drink made from the dried shredded leaves of an Asian shrub and hot water.

Taybrak: Short sojourn from work for some refreshment.

Tear Lumps Aff: Give a severe dressing-down to.

Tearin' Wan Anoller: Violent altercation (usually between children).

Teem: Drain off excess water from boiling potatoes.

Tell Iz Sumfin' We Don't Know: I know that.

Tendy Wan Faverit: The horse or greyhound that's certain to win the race.

That Bitts Banagher An' Banagher Bitt The Divil: A nine-day wonder that lasts for ten.

That Boy: Sneering reference to disliked male, regardless of age.

That Crowd: Usually adverse reference to all government bodies.

That Oul Brute: That uncouth male.

That Wud Fit Finn Ma Cool: I think your clothes are a bit too big for you.

That'll Fatten Ye: That won't fatten you at all – nor will it benefit you.

That'll Giv Ye Warts: Reprimand to child not to let air from balloon blow on to her/his face.

That'll Niver Buy The Wane A Coat: That's not much good.

That's A Sin: You shouldn't be doing whatever it is you're doing.

That's Anoller Sharp Wan: Is there no end to this cold weather?

That's Fur Me Ti Know An' You Ti Fine Out: I know but I'm certainly not telling you.

That's Gran': I'm happy that we can agree.

That's In Front Ay Sumfin': Said when someone deviates from usual behaviour.

That's My Excuse, Wat's Yurs? You're just as bad as me.

That's My Story An' Am Stickin' Ti It: Weak excuse put forward by person when it's obvious to everyone that he's lying.

That's Orr Ite Fur You: I don't care about you, what about me?

That's Wile Nice A Ye: Thanks for nothing.

That's You Toul Aff: Sympathetic consolation after verbal rebuke.

The Balls A May Legs Are Turned Ti The Front: My legs are very sore.

The Blether's Niver Far From Yur Eyes: You're always near to tears.

The Bror: My brother.

The Cat Can Luk At The King: Sharp retort to the question 'What are you looking at?'

The Crows Wur Puttin' Out Thur Tongues Wi' Heat: The temperature was abnormally high.

The Cruelty Man: Person responsible for child welfare.

The Divil's Lukin' Outta Yur Eyes: Said by parent to child in an attempt to scare it into changing its naughty ways.

The Gimmeys: Affliction that makes people (especially children) keep asking for things.

The Gravy's Lashin' A May: I'm very hot; I'm sweating profusely.

The Hen That Laid Them Must've Had Stays On: Those eggs are rather small.

The Holy Man's Name: A religious oath.

The Kinda May: The type of person I am.

The Messages: The groceries; shopping.

The Morra: The day after today.

The Nash: National assistance – a type of unemployment benefit no longer in use.

The Nurls: Chickenpox.

The Reek Wudda Knocked Ye Down: There was an awful stench.

The Saftest Thing About That Boy Is His Teeth: He's not as innocent as he lets on.

The Snotters Wuz Trippin' Im: His nose needed cleaning.

The Stitt: The Republic of Ireland.

The Stitts: Huge country on the other side of the Atlantic, just south of Canada.

The Things Ye See When Ye Hivn't A Gun: Jovial insult on a chance meeting with an old friend.

The Tune The Oul Cow Died Wi': Sound emanating from 'singers' bereft of melody and tone.

The Two Mahoods: Two friends or associates who are always together.

The Voice In The Wulderness: Sound of person speaking up in a futile attempt to draw attention to a problem.

Them Bokeys'll Mik A Rope An' Drag Ye Down In Ti The Quay: Dire warning from parent to child of what will befall them if they refuse to have their hair fine-combed.

Them Cups Hiv Beards On Them: That china needs washing.

Them Oul Derry Wans: Light-hearted reference by 'outsiders' to inhabitants of the Maiden City.

Them There/Themins: Those people.

There'll Be Two Blue Moons In The Sky An' Wan In The Dungpit: That's unlikely to occur.

There's May Han' Up Ti God: I swear it's the truth.

There's More Beef On A Coul Chip: I've seen better built people.

There's More John Orrs Than Wan John Orr: There's more than one person with the same name.

There's Nawhin' Ti Ail Ye: You're quite capable of doing it yourself.

There's Wiser In Lukin' Out: A belief that someone is not in full control of their senses.

They'd Tik The Bite Outta Yur Mouth: They're greedy people.

Thick/Thick As Poundies: Stupid.

Things Are Lukin' Black In The Coalmine: Jovial term saying that all isn't well.

Thon Donor: That stupid old so-and-so.

Thon Wan: That person.

Thon's Hit: That's it.

Thonder: Over there.

Thote: Cylindrical part of body between head and trunk which facilitates the passage of food and air.

Thran: Obstinate; hard to shift.

Thrapple: Throat or Adam's apple.

Threatenin' Letter: Written notification from the labour exchange (Jobmarket) about a job opportunity.

Threble: Threefold; optimistic bet in turf accountant's requiring three horses, dogs or teams to win.

Three Dee Orinje: Lemonade drink from Wee Johnny's shop, formerly in Bishop Street.

Throw The Head: Completely lose control; go berserk.

Throw Yursel Tigether: Dress yourself quickly, we are going out now.

Thru Goin': Description of unmanageable child.

Thur Neck's Broke: Description of extremely spoiled children.

Thur's More Hair On A Billiard Ball: Unkind remark passed to male who is slightly thin on top.

Thurday: Two and a half dozen.

Ti Hell Wi' Obcastin': Some things are better left unsaid.

Tibble: Square wooden piece of furniture with four legs.

Tick: Credit given in shops etc.

Tie The Boy: Character renowned for his untidy manner of dress.

Tik A Fit: Recoil in shock at unwelcome news or event.

Tik Down: Defame someone's character; maliciously criticise.

Tik The Bare Luk Off: Do something to divert attention from; to dress something up a bit.

Tik The Break Off: Create distraction to lessen the embarrassment.

Tik The Good Outta: Perform a generous act then negate it by doing something mean.

Tik The Heart From Ye: Compliment on noticing an appetising aroma.

Tik The Rough Off: Give a light cleaning; spruce up slightly.

Tik Up: About to change for the better (eg I think the weller's about to tik up).

Tik Yur Shade: To pinch the nose and dip the head backwards under the water when swimming (said by children).

Tikkin' A Wile Han' At: Making a fool of; joking with.

Tikkin In: Being admitted to hospital.

Tikkit Thick: Respond unfavourably to joke or prank.

Till (The Durr): Push the door ajar.

Tilly: Daily Belfast newspaper.

Tip's Yur Keek: Game of street football in which even a slight touch of the ball is considered a kick.

Tipp Acordur: Electronic device for recording sound.

Tizz: It is.

Tizzn't: It isn't.

Tom The Divil Cudn't Scar Ye: Why don't you drop the pretence of being afraid?

Tongue Hingin' Out: Dying of thirst; green with envy.

Toothick: Intense pain in the nerves of the mouth, instigating an unwelcome visit to the dentist.

Top: Little handle in sink for turning water off and on.

Tortured: Repeatedly irritated by another's behaviour.

Tossie Pit: Group of people gambling by flipping coins in the air.

Touch: Accost for a loan of some money.

Touched: Slightly off balance mentally.

Toul Ti The Bone A Yur Nose: Told off straight to your face, with no punches pulled.

Toul: Told; imparted information to.

Trail: Fight; drag along by the hair.

Trailin': Setting out on an unrewarding errand.

Triller: Small cart affair towed behind vehicle; short preview of film.

Trimendus: Great; excellent.

Trimmlin': Shaking with fear or cold.

Trowses: Long pants.

Trumf: Trumps (as in cards).

Tube 'N' Cover: Old-style soccer ball.

Tuffy: Hard confectionery.

Tuk Bad: Became ill.

Tuk Wake: Felt faint; overcome with sickness or nerves.

Tummle: Topple over.

Turmit: Large root vegetable.

Turn On Yur Heel: Abruptly leave and bring conversation to an end.

Turn Roun': Begin, usually unfavourably.

Turn: Be converted to another religion.

Twenny: Four short of two dozen.

Two Burnt Holes In A Blanket: Descriptive of eyes after a night of little sleep or heavy drinking.

Two Hairs Past A Freckle: I haven't a clue what time it is, I haven't got a watch.

Two On Ti Wan Kills A Man: Uneven contest.

Two Wanses: Two tossed coins landing with one showing heads and the other tails.

Two's Up On Ye: Request for smoke of cigarette.

Twust: Bend out of shape; early sixties dance.

Twyste: Two times.

U–V

Ukalily: Small guitar-shaped musical instrument with four strings.

Unknownst Ti Me: Without my knowledge or consent.

Up A Tree In Rosemount: Missing but not missed; whereabouts unknown, absence unlamented.

Up My Back Fur A Hump: I don't know where it is and I don't care.

Up The Country: Anywhere in Ireland outside Derry.

Up The Wudden Hill: Where children go to get to bed.

Up Ti Belfast: Down to Belfast.

Usual Oul Toot: Same old story.

Vennel: Pipe for water to drain away.

Vepes: VP wine.

Vile-o: One who was completely forgotten when good looks and other attractive attributes were handed out.

Viper: Backbiter; one whose veracity is suspect.

Voice Lik A Foghorn: Not exactly dulcet toned; of a gruff vocal nature.

Famous Derry Places
(Past and Present)

Altygalvin: Derry's main hospital.

Back Of The Wall: Nailor's Row/ Walker's Square area, now demolished.

The Back Stores: Alleyway that once went from Little James Street to William Street.

Bap's: Battisti's Café, once situated in Ferryquay Street.

The Basin: Creggan Reservoir.

The Big House: The old asylum on the Strand Road.

The Bloods: Old dancehall in the Bogside.

Breeze Lane: Road between Lone Moor Road and Creggan.

Bridge Street University: Little school in Bridge Street, now closed.

Bucket Of Blood: Public house infamous for brawls, once situated at Bishop's Gate.

The Bug Ranch: Old City Cinema once in William Street.

The Bull: Area on the Lone Moor Rd.

The Byewash: Little waterfall between Rosemount and Glenowen.

Cannibal Island: Rinmore Drive in Creggan.

The Close: Small street once situated in the Rossville Street area.

The Cropie: Roundabout at junction of Central Drive and Westway in Creggan.

The Dark Lane: Small street once in the Long Tower area, now demolished.

The Donkey/Daisy Fields: Grassy areas in the Brandywell area.

The Dump: Football pitch in the Brandywell area.

Egglington: Picturesque village not far from Derry.

The Five Lamps: Toilets once in Waterloo Place.

The Fryin' Pan: Small pub once situated on the Lone Moor Road.

Futta Stanley's: At the bottom of Stanley's Walk, a street in the Bogside.

The Gashyard: The former gasworks on the Lecky Road.

The Gorbals: The Waterside.

Grazy Barney's: Little fish and chip shop once situated in William Street.

Greenhell: Springtown Camp, former US forces base in WWII, no longer in existence.

The Heights: The top end of the Creggan Estate.

Hogg's Folly: Steep winding street in the Long Tower area.

Holy Rosemount: Area situated near Creggan Estate.

Ivy House: A tall red-bricked building formerly beside the old Strand Cinema.

Jerusalem: Meenan Park.

Molly On The Moor: Second-hand shop that used to be on the Lone Moor Road.

Thran John's: Public house in Shantallow.

The Threepenny Bits: Stone fixtures that used to be in front of the Rossville Street flats.

Thunderin' Down: Narrow lane off Lone Moor Road, now demolished.

Top Of The Hill: Gobnascale.

Treacle Hole's: Shop in Central Drive.

Up The Bankin': Grassy slope between the Bogside and Derry's Walls.

Up The Bog: Somewhere in the Bogside.

Up The Boleyays: Area in Waterside associated with romantic assignations.

Wee Johnny's: Old-fashioned 'swiddie' shop that used to be in Bishop Street.

The Workhouse: Grim building now refurbished as the Waterside Library.

W

Wa? I didn't hear you; say it again.

Wabblin' Brush: Implement for applying shaving soap to the face.

Wadgin: Big, shapeless piece of something.

Wagon: Derogatory term from yesteryear descriptive of female with less than attractive features.

Wait An' Al Buy Ye A Dummy Tit: Don't be such a baby.

Wait An' I'll Dance Ti Ye: I certainly will not do as you ask.

Walter: Play around in mud or dirt.

Wan: One.

Wan A Yese: One at a time, please.

Wan Bitta Harm (Didn't Do May): Had no detrimental effect.

Wan Poun' Wan: One guinea in pre-decimalisation days.

Wan Word From Me An' He Does Wat He Liks: Admission by parent that he/she has little control over a child.

Wan Yeer Oul: One year old.

Wan's Errand: Fruitless message.

Wanebitter: Person who picks fights with kids.

Wanes: Children.

Want A Tista Salt? Hint to someone to stop biting their nails.

Warewulf: Mythical creature who allegedly could change from a man into a horrible lupine monster.

Warped Jute: Weirdo.

Wash Yur Mouth Out Wi' Soap An' Holy Watter: There's no need for all that profanity.

Waster: A good-for-nothing individual.

Wat About Ye, Kid? Warm greeting to a good friend.

Wat Did Yur Last Skivvy Die Of? Do it yourself.

Wat Iver Ye Say, Say Nawhin' (Ti Ye See Claude): Refrain from talking until you consult a solicitor; plead innocent.

Wat Possessed Ye? Why did you act the way you did?

Wat Size De Ye Wear? Would you mind stamping out my cigarette butt?

Watch The Grittins: Helpful but teasing advice to thin person.

Watch The Material: Please keep your hands off my new suit.

Watch Ye Don't Heat Yur Watter: Sarcastic remark to slowcoach.

Watch Ye Don't Loss Yur Finger: Would you please stop picking your nose.

Wat's Bitin' Yur Cookie? What's the matter?

Wat's That, A Scotch Mist? Rebuke by someone who asks another to find something without success then finds it himself.

Wat's The Craic? Any news? What's happening?

Wat's The Damage? How much do I owe you?

Wat's Yur Beef? What is it you wish to complain about?

Watta Nunder God's That? Shocked reaction to loud noise or unusual sound.

Watter: Clear liquid used for drinking and washing; H_2O.

Watter Biscuits: Cream crackers.

Watterbrash: Indigestion; sour acid from stomach.

Way A Goin' On: General, everyday manner.

We All Hiv Wur Wee Ways A Goin' Mad: Sarcastic answer by someone who has just had one of their little eccentric foibles pointed out.

We Know Ye Are: You are not.

We Know Ye: Smug remark made when someone's darkest secret is discovered.

We Niver Died A Winter Yit: Cheer up! Things can only get worse.

Wee Article: Cheeky, forward child.

Wee Bibby: Very young child.

Wee Birdie: Light kiss.

Wee Buns: Very easy; no problem.

Wee Critter: Expression of sympathy for suffering child or animal.

Wee Curt: Pleasant little cuddle with member of the opposite sex.

Wee Dote: Compliment to a cute baby; term of endearment used by a girl about a good-looking boy.

Wee Feel: A little romantic messing around.

Wee Hard: Small tough person.

Wee Hitler: Small upstart who has a modicum of power over the general public (eg Traffic Warden).

Wee Lick: Light dusting; quick wash.

Wee Matney Coat: Little garment for the child.

Wee Minute: Short period of time; normally longer than a minute.

Wee Nadger: Term for youngest or smallest in the family.

Wee Nuns: Primary school in the vicinity of the Long Tower Church, Derry.

Wee People: Children; young adults.

Wee Pitcher: Supporting film in cinema.

Wee Reek: Furtive smoke of cigarette.

Wee Rub: Light embrocation, usually Vicks, designed to alleviate chest congestion associated with bad weather.

Wee Scrip: A quick shave.

Wee Sope/Drop In Yur Han': Quick drink of tea offered to a visitor, not in the hand but in a cup.

Wee Tist: A little of anything.

Wee Wane Wi' An Oul Woman's Head: Description of child too advanced for its years.

Wee Want: Something missing mentally in a person.

Wee Way A Workin': Routine peculiar to each individual.

Weemin: Adult females.

Ween: A small number; a few.

Well At: Wealthy.

Well Away: Going great; doing very well.

Well Mended: Having put on weight; physically improved.

Well Turned Out: Neatly presented; smartly dressed.

Welltin Street: Area of Bogside no longer in existence.

Whaddy Ye Doin' This Weller? Have you found employment?

Whaddy Ye Hink It Is – Christmas? No, you can't have it.

Whaddy Ye Want – Blud? Do you not think you've taken enough from me?

Whaddy Ye Want Fur Nawhin'? You're lucky you're getting what you're getting.

When Hunger Comes In The Durr, Pride Flies Out The Wunda: Poor people have to accept charity.

When Ye Put On Yur Shoes In The Mornin', Ye Niver Know Who'll Tik them Off: You can't be sure when you're going to die.

When Yur Han's In: Now that you've got the hang of it.

Where De Ye Burry Yur Dead? You're full of hot air; you think you are tough but I disagree.

Where's Yur Office? Mind your own business; don't try to boss me about.

Whinging: Insistent quiet crying or moaning.

Whisperin' Man: Mysterious character, infamous for knocking at (or peeping in) people's windows.

Who Eye Ye On Fur? Who do you support?

Who Owns Ye Yo Ho? Expression of disbelief.

Who's Yur Man? Who does he think he is?

Whole Mouthful: Barrage of profanity; a string of oaths.

Whole Tribe: A very large family.

Why Don't Ye Bring Yur Bed Wi' Ye? Advice to person who's caught laying down on the job.

Why Don't Ye Put It In A Glass Kis An' Throw Sugar At It? Facetious advice given to someone who is overprotective about one of their possessions.

Wi'out A Dollion: Completely naked.

Widder: Person in restaurant who serves up the meals.

Wig: Pull someone's hair.

Wile: Very; terrible.

Wile About: Madly in love with.

Wile Bad: Very ill.

Wile Big Connection: Large circle of family and friends.

Wile Big Eyed: Greedy.

Wile Blowey: Windy; blowing a gale.

Wile Bouncy: Very springy (as of bed).

Wile Civil: Good-natured; decent type.

Wile Clatter A Wanes: A family many in number and young in years.

Wile Colour/Wile Pisty Lukin': Sick looking; having a wan complexion/appearance.

Wile Curse: Terribly uncouth; very rough around the edges.

Wile Dose: A cold or flu.

Wile Footery: Small and hard to work with; person who works in an irritating manner.

Wile Fur: Has a strong inclination to.

Wile Good Livin': Leading a pious life.

Wile Keekin': To suffer or inflict a serious assault.

Wile Kis: Humorous, outgoing sort of person.

Wile Lukin': Ugly.

Wile Man: Mischievous, unpredictable, devil-may-care person.

Wile Messer: Someone incapable of acting in a responsible and decisive manner.

Wile Neck: Having no sense of embarrassment or shame.

Wile Slippy: Very slippery.

Wile Strange: Child who doesn't take to strangers.

Wile Stuck: In need of immediate cash or other commodity.

Wile Ti Luk At: Unbearable performance of artist or football team.

Wile Tik A Han': Person who plays tricks on, or makes fun of, others.

Wile Wist: Pointless squandering of resources.

Wile Witt: Extremely heavy.

Wile Wundy Weller: Extremely unsettled climatic conditions.

Wine Victim: Sad name for a person who's too fond of cheap alcohol.

Wing: One penny in 'old' money.

Winna Han'? May I be of assistance?

Wiped: Having dole money stopped in contentious circumstances.

Wired Up Ti The Moon: Psychologically disturbed.

Wise Up, Wull Ye? Have some sense.

Wistcoat: Short, tight, sleeveless jacket.

Wistin': Frittering away (eg wistin' time).

Wo, Beek: Command for horse to stop.

Won't Try A Leg: Makes no attempt at all; lazy.

Wooden Overcoat: Coffin.

Work A Lyin' Week: Toil for seven days in lieu of wages.

Work A Wee Move: Pull off a coup.

Work In: Get some overtime on the job.

Worked Wi': Brought round; helped to recover after a shock or accident.

Worser: Said of any situation that has deteriorated enough to cause concern.

Wreck The House: Name for clumsy person; cheap wine.

Wrecked: Extremely embarrassed; very drunk.

Wrong Sort: Not of the proper religious persuasion.

Wud Ye Be Guilty? You wouldn't catch me doing that.

Wud Ye Lik May Ti Dance Ye A Jig? Who do you think you're trying to boss about?

Wud Ye Mind Where You're Puttin' Yur Big Size Tens: Mind your feet.

Wud Ye Tik May Grave As Quick? Question asked when someone 'steals' another's seat.

Wud Ye Tik That Oul Fis Off Ye: For God's sake, cheer up.

Wudd: Material trees are made from.

Wudda Woman: A lady whose husband has passed away.

Wudn't Turn The Word In Yur Mouth: Very docile; wouldn't argue back.

Wull: Fleece of sheep used for knitting jumpers etc.

Wulla? Will I?

Wullered: Dried-up and drooping.

Wully Winkle: Santa Claus's sidekick who, for a few weeks before Christmas, checks to see that children are in bed at a reasonable hour; seasonal Peeping Tom.

Wulwurs: Large department store, formerly in central Derry.

Wumman's Pitcher: Film more suited to the ladies; tear-jerker.

Wun: Fast moving air.

Wunbush: Little shrub that grows in fields and along hedgerows.

Wunda: A gap covered in glass in a building which permits light and air to enter and people inside to view what is outside.

Wunst: Once upon a time.

Wunter: The coldest season of the year.

Wupp: Long leather implement used for encouraging horses to run faster, or for flogging people.

Wur: Our, where, were, or we're.

Wur Ill Ley? I wonder where they've got to?

Wur Qwuts: We are now on equal terms.

Wur Ye Born In A Fiel' Ur Wat?: Close that door.

Wur Ye In The Bookies? Question designed to draw attention to the fact the lady's slip is showing.

Wur Ye Out Wunda Cleanin'? Dear me, you've got a ladder in your stocking.

Wurl: Wheel along; spinning wildly.

Wursels: Us; we people.

Wush Ye Wur As Good At Sayin' Yur Prayers: Said when someone disapproves of another's actions.

Wuspur: Quiet word in the ear.

Wussle: High frequency sound emitted from mouth; referee's instrument for controlling game.

Wutniss: Person called by court to testify; one who is present at some event.

Wuttlin': Carving little shapes out of wood (usually with a penknife).

Wuz Ay Wearin' Dark Glasses? Jibe by girl when friend has just announced that someone fancies her.

Y

Yahoo: Rowdy but usually harmless character.

Ye Big Girl, Ye: Don't be such a drip.

Ye Can Stan' There Ti Yur Googy Wuthers: There's not much point in you hanging round here.

Ye Cud Grow Spuds In Yur Ears: Why don't you wash yourself more often?

Ye Cud See A Flay Walkin' Up Yur Leg: Observation that a person's trousers are a bit on the tight side.

Ye Cudn't Bay Up Ti Ye: You're worth the watching.

Ye Cudn't Beat Snow Ay A Rope/ Casey's Drum: Sneering retort to someone who threatens violence.

Ye Cudn't Box Eggs: You aren't exactly Mohammed Ali.

Ye Cudn't Break Ye Wi' A Sledgehammer: You're not easily embarrassed.

Ye Cudn't Draw The Bru: You're not a very good artist.

Ye Cudn't Hear Yur Ears: It was too noisy.

Ye Cudn't Keek A Hen Ti Death/ Ye Cudn't Pass Yur Watter: What a terrible footballer you are.

Ye Cudn't Lik Im If He Wuz Made A Chocolate: He's not a very nice person.

Ye Cudn't Lik Ye If Ye Wur After Hivin' Ye: You're the most hateful individual I know.

Ye Cudn't Run A Raffle A Pan-cakes: Your aptitude for organisation leaves a lot to be desired.

Ye Cudn't See Green Cheese But Yur Mouth Watters: You're a very greedy person.

Ye Cudn't Throw Up: Severe criticism of incompetent dart thrower.

Ye Cudn't Work In A Fit: Toiling isn't one of your strong points.

Ye Don't Hiv A Good Word Ti Say Bout Nobody: I suppose you're whiter than white.

Ye Don't Want Much, De Ye? Do you not think you've set your sights a bit high?

Ye Hiv Two Chances: You've absolutely no chance at all.

Ye Know: You don't know – that's why I'm telling you.

Ye Know Wat I Mean, Lik? Do you get the message?

Ye May Mik Do: I'm afraid you'll have to make the best of what you've got.

Ye Member Yur Granny Well: You've got a good memory.

Ye Missed It: You should have been there for the merriment and other wonderful goings-on.

Ye Must Bay Hard Up Fur A Bite: You'd eat anything, wouldn't you?

Ye Nearly Had A Fry: Hard luck, old boy.

Ye Niver Go Nowhere: Admonishment to person who fails to fulfil his Christian duties.

Ye Niver Know You're Livin' Ti Ye Luk At Yur Shirt: You learn something new every day.

Ye Niver Toul May That Bar: Why did you fail to divulge that important piece of information?

Ye Say More Than Yur Prayers: You're nothing but a bluffer.

Ye Tell Me That, Aye? I'm not sure if I believe you.

Ye Tuk That Outta May This Day: Words of rebuke to child by swearing parent.

Ye Wudn't Git Peace Ti Do Nawhin': Is there no end to these interruptions?

Ye'd Bay Litt Fur Yur Own Funeril: Your tardiness is quite unacceptable.

Ye'd Git Redd A Yur Smell That Day: It's very windy outside today.

Ye'd Hink A Bomb Hit This Pliss: Reference to untidy house.

Ye'd Hink All The Cats In Derry Wuz Chewin' At Yur Hair: Insensitive remark passed to someone who has just had a new hairdo (especially a modern one).

Ye'd Hink Sumwan Hit Ye Up The Bake Wi' A Bag A Flour: Why do you wear so much face powder?

Ye'd Hink The Dead Lice Wuz Fallin' Aff Ye: God, but you're a lazy good-for-nothing.

Ye'd Hink Ye Niver Washed Fur A Week: Your personal hygiene leaves a lot to be desired.

Ye'd Hink Ye Wur Vaccinated Wi' A Gramophone Needle: Would you please stop talking for a moment.

Ye'd Luk Well: You'd look very foolish.

Ye'd Need A Pixie On Ye That Weller: It's extremely cold today.

Ye'll Bay All Right In The Mornin', Sure: Why are you acting so strange?

Ye'll Bay Bringin' Them Out Lit Nixt: Jibe directed at miser who has just secretly ignited a cigarette without offering any to others.

Ye'll Bay Pickin' Leller Outta Yur Ass Fur A Week: I'm about to administer you a hefty kick.

Ye'll Hit Whose Granny Wi' A Wine Bottle? Jocular remark to mock threat of assault on one's person.

Ye'll Hiv A Long Witt: I wouldn't hold my breath if I were you.

Ye'll Niver Hiv Luck: Bemoaning what was considered the dubious good fortune of another.

Ye've A Brass Neck On Ye/Ye've A Neck Lik Nelson: You've got a nerve.

Ye've Got Yur Gittins: You've had enough; you're getting no more.

Ye've Neller Manners Nur Breedin': You're as common as muck.

Ye've No Ern: You haven't a hope in hell.

Yella: Bright pastel colour; cowardly.

Yes: Puzzling answer to unasked question, used as a greeting when one Derry person meets another.

Yes, Boss: Greeting to someone who's not your employer.

Yisterey: The day before today.

Yock: Awkward person at work; anything old and dilapidated.

You Giv Me The Pip: You annoy me.

You Wud Know: You definitely would not know.

You Wurn't Behine The Durr When They Wur Given Out Eller, Wur Ye? Common retort when someone makes a remark about some part of another's anatomy.

You'd Kill Dead Things: You're all talk and no action.

You'd Lik Ti Know: I'm not telling you.

You'll Dear Buy It: You're in for it; there's trouble brewing.

You'll Eat Hit B'fore Hit Eats You: Admonishment to child who sulks and won't eat.

You're A Good Turn: What do you take me for? Do you expect me to believe you?

You're A Good Turn But There's A Better Wan In Yur Eye: You are not fooling me; I see through you.

You're A Good Un But You'll Go: Patronising remark.

You're A Liar: You don't say – tell me some more.

You're A Teller: I know you don't really work in a bank, but is what you've just said true?

You're A Wile Bad Wunda/ Standin' In May Light: Would you please stop obstructing my view.

You're Away Wi' The Fairies: You are not making any sense; telling unbelievable stories.

You're Better Ravin' There Than In Yur Bed: You're talking complete rubbish.

You're Excused But You're Dammed Ignernt: Expression of mocking forgiveness.

You're Funny But Yur Fis Beats Ye: That's not a bit funny.

You're Fur Nawhin': Person totally without merit; a waster.

You're Good Crack At A Wake: You're not at all funny.

You're In Fur It: Warning to child there's a hiding in store from parents.

You're Laughin': You're home and dry; success is imminent.

You're Lik Haff-Hung McNutt: Straighten your collar and tie.

You're Lukin' At: This is what it will cost you.

You're Lukin' Well, Were Ye Lyin'? You look terrible, what happened to you?

You're Mad So Ye Are: That was a stupid thing to do.

You're No Dozer: It would be difficult to fool you.

You're Not G'in Out Lik That, Eye Ye? Do you not think you could dress a little better on social occasions? (Usually directed at husband from wife.)

You're Not On: Nothing doing; no way!

You're Quare An' Green: Don't try to kid me.

You're Some Boy, Hi: Expression of disappointment when let down by friend.

You're Wile, So Ye Are: Oh, you're absolutely awful.

You're Yur Da/Ma In The Sod: Observation that child behaves like parent.

Youse/Yese/Yousins: You people.

Yungfla: Common term applied to male, regardless of age.

Yur Bum's Out The Wunda: You're wrong; you've had it.

Yur Eye's Out: You've no chance; someone else will beat you to it.

Yur Granny Wuz Doherty (An' She Wuz The Blud): Regardless of who your granny was, you're wrong.

Yur Head's A Marley: I think you've reached an incorrect conclusion; you're talking rubbish.

Yur Head's Cut: I disagree with you.

Yur Head's Full A Sweedie Mice: You're completely out of touch with reality.

Yur Head's Lik A Busby: You're in need of a haircut.

Yur Own's No Miss: You are equally unsymmetrical in body shape.

Yur Socks Need Soled An' Heeled: It's time you were changing your hosiery.

Yur Tube's Out: You haven't a hope.

Yur Wants Wud Make A Poor Man Rich: There's no pleasing you.

The Great Derry Quiz

**Do you have the qualities to be a fully fledged citizen of Derry?
Answer the questions below and find out.**

Fur Men

1. Can you eat at least half a dozen baps at the one sitting?
Yes ☐ **No** ☐

2. Can you push a pram with one hand, with your free hand in your back pocket, trying to look as if you don't do it all the time? **Yes** ☐ **No** ☐

3. Can you smoke a quarter-inch butt without burning your fingers?
Yes ☐ **No** ☐

4. Are you a pub-quiz addict and spend your spare time memorising all the capital cities of the world and the winners of the European Cup since 1955? **Yes** ☐ **No** ☐

5. Do you spend at least six hours a week in the bookies or at a card school? **Yes** ☐ **No** ☐

6. Have you ever received an invitation to the Bru's annual dance?
Yes ☐ **No** ☐

7. Have you ever been photographed for the 'Derry Journal' with either a mayor or a wile big cheque?
Yes ☐ **No** ☐

8. Have you ever had a request played on Radio Foyle for 'anyone that knows me'? **Yes** ☐ **No** ☐

9. Do you use the words 'mucker' or 'yes, hi' regularly? **Yes** ☐ **No** ☐

10. Are you in the Cursillo Movement and walk to Knock every year?
Yes ☐ **No** ☐

11. Have you ever owned, or even walked, a greyhound? **Yes** ☐ **No** ☐

12. Have you ever gathered brock or sold sticks? **Yes** ☐ **No** ☐

13. When asked to sing in a pub, do you render either 'Starry Night', 'The Candy Store' or, even worse, both?
Yes ☐ **No** ☐

14. Do you wear white socks and black slip-ons, and if over thirty, are you always five years behind the latest fashions? **Yes** ☐ **No** ☐

15. Have you ever gone to England for a fortnight and returned with an English accent? **Yes** ☐ **No** ☐

16. Can you dance the 'Corinthian Crawl' or have you tried to jive to 'rave' music? **Yes** ☐ **No** ☐

17. Have you ever 'scranned' a few bob from your ma? **Yes** ☐ **No** ☐

18. Do you prefer to watch Derry City from the College Field or the graveyard rather than the Brandy itself? **Yes** ☐ **No** ☐

19. Are you still convinced that the 'Showbands' are about to make a comeback? **Yes** ☐ **No** ☐

20. Did you have at least wan bayten docket this week? **Yes** ☐ **No** ☐

21. Do you continually (or deliberately) forget your spouse's name and refer to her as 'the wife'? **Yes** ☐ **No** ☐

Fur Weemin

1. Can you run with your arms folded, with absolutely no movement of the chest? **Yes** ☐ **No** ☐

2. Can you sit cross-legged, tucking the toes of the upper leg behind the calf of the lower leg? **Yes** ☐ **No** ☐

3. Do you actively seek out the latest scandal or 'bars'? **Yes** ☐ **No** ☐

4. Do you wear your curlers and house slippers to bingo? **Yes** ☐ **No** ☐

5. Do you like apple turnovers or a 'lodger'? **Yes** ☐ **No** ☐

6. Do you hate visiting your in-laws on Saturdays so as he can get his ma's stews? **Yes** ☐ **No** ☐

7. Do you prefer to live, at most, two doors from your mother? **Yes** ☐ **No** ☐

8. Do you have a female child named either Kylie or Rihanna? **Yes** ☐ **No** ☐

9. Have you ever referred to a would-be suitor as a 'tube'? **Yes** ☐ **No** ☐

10. Have you ever worked in a shirt factory and occasionally slunk off in the afternoon to go to the matinée with your bars? **Yes** ☐ **No** ☐

11. Can you exhale a cloud of cigarette smoke and at the same time make a loud crack with a chewing-gum bubble? **Yes** ☐ **No** ☐

12. When invited to sing in a pub or at a party, is your repertoire limited to 'One Day At A Time' or 'Harper Valley PTA'? **Yes** ☐ **No** ☐

13. Can you jive with one hand while holding your skirt down with the other and simultaneously smoking a fag? **Yes** ☐ **No** ☐

14. Are you at least two months behind on your Credit Union book? **Yes** ☐ **No** ☐

15. Was the highlight of your week a Sunday night in St Eugene's Parish Hall with your mates and a wee carry-out? **Yes** ☐ **No** ☐

16. Are you an avid listener of Sean Coyle's Radio Foyle show? **Yes** ☐ **No** ☐

17. Did you ever back-comb your hair and spray it with lacquer before heading off to Borderland on the bus to see Dickie Rock?

Yes ☐ No ☐

18. Do you still hanker for the days when the Yanks were here?

Yes ☐ No ☐

19. Do you allow a man to put his hands inside your coat in cold weather when courting?

Yes ☐ No ☐

20. Do you know the words of 'The Town I Loved So Well' off by heart?

Yes ☐ No ☐

21. Have you ever put an ad in the 'Derry Journal' that said: 'Lordy, Lordy, Look who's 40!'?

Yes ☐ No ☐

How did you score?

Twenty-one – Congratulations. You're the perfect Derry Wan. Tell the world.

Fifteen to twenty – You're highly commended and definitely in with a shout with a bit more practice.

pass mark pass mark pass mark pass mark pass mark pass mark pass mark pass mark

Ten to fourteen – Nearly there, hitting the bar, try a little harder and you'll make it.

Six to nine – I'm afraid you'll have to pull your (white) socks up or spend more time with Sean Coyle if you want to be a serious contender.

Three to five – The chances of you ever achieving full Derry status, unfortunately, are slim indeed. Try eating more baps and get a lifetime subscription to the 'Derry Journal'.

Less than three – **No way, José!** Major disaster! Forget it and try a lesser place like Strabane.

If you've passed, then congratulations, well done, good job. Now collect your certificate opposite and go spread the word.

If you've failed, then tough!

The University of Guilthall Press

VITA · VERITAS · VICTORIA

By virtue of us all being full ay wursels and by being far too clever by half fur wur own boots, the university has this day conferred the degree of

True Derryhood

on

. . . .

having completed a course in the study of Derryisms, including an intensive study of *The Wile Big Derry Phrasebook* and successful completion of the final examination.

Signed on behalf of the University . . . .

Seamus McConnell
Honorary Chancer